Letters
TO MY
DAUGHTERS

BUSINESS
ADVICE FOR
ENTREPRENEURS

Linda Hollyer, MBA

LINDA HOLLYER
Letters to My Daughters—Business Advice for Entrepreneurs

ISBN
978-1-7753932-0-7 (Print Book)
978-1-7753932-1-4 (E-Book)
978-1-7753932-2-1 (Audio Book)

EDITOR Lori Bamber
BOOK DESIGN Jazmin Welch
COVER PHOTOGRAPHY Hannah Martin Photography
AUTHOR PORTRAIT Hannah McFall Photography
PUBLISHING SUPPORT The Self Publishing Agency

▌ DEDICATION

I wish my father, Roger Marion, were here to see what his work has created. As you will read in this book, the many entrepreneurial and life lessons he shared with me have guided my career as well as my growth as a person.

My dad was my biggest cheerleader, and always expected and got the very best from me. Every day, I see his optimism and energy living on in my three daughters and me.

In many ways, the book you're holding is a letter from him to all of us.

Linda Hollzer

TABLE OF CONTENTS

INTRODUCTION

In the spring of 2016, I gazed out the window of my luxurious hotel room, over the scenic city of Amsterdam, and thought about how far I was from the people I love.

Thirty or so years into a successful corporate and start-up career, and after building two lucrative, respected companies, I was a 50-something-year-old woman attending one more trade show with thousands of techies, mostly men in their 20s, 30s and early 40s. I'd already visited 42 countries for work, many of them more than once, and the thrill of business travel was gone.

Missing my husband, my kids, my friends and my home, I suddenly knew this stage of my life was coming to an end. I returned home with a plan to wind down my business and started thinking about what I'd do next.

I've always wanted to write about the many lessons I'd learned during my career in business and from my father, one of the original entrepreneurs. It wasn't long before my dream intersected with the dreams of one of my three daughters, Danielle.

Danielle had recently launched an amazing networking group for millennial women in Vancouver, our hometown, and she asked me if I'd consider helping her. As I got to know these inspiring young women, I realized that—while a lot has changed since I started out in my 20s, particularly in technology—some things remain the same. Women still have to work harder to stand out and be taken seriously; they continue to do more than their fair share of work outside work, leaving less time and energy for networking and education; and they still experience a severe shortage of female role models and mentors with time to spare. In other words, they need help.

Over the years, I've spent countless hours on the phone talking through career and business challenges with my entrepreneurial daughters. It occurred to me that every young female entrepreneur needs a mom who has built successful businesses, but most don't have one. I wondered—what if I could share what I'd learned with them as well?

This question inspired the book you now hold in your hands. Without judgment or intimidation—no jargon or jockeying for ego points—my aim is to equip the many women who are starting businesses with the basics they need to succeed.

Whether you are deep into your start-up and working 18 hours a day programming a new app or you're thinking about starting an Etsy business that will allow you to pay some bills while spending time with your young children, *Letters to my Daughters* is for you. It's a caring, straightforward look at the problems everyone in business will face at some point, with a particular focus on the issues women tend to experience.

Being an entrepreneur is a long, tough road—you won't succeed if you're not willing to work hard, learn constantly and build resilience. But the rewards are unbeatable, too, and you don't have to do it alone.

The chapters inside are brief and to the point, as I know from experience you don't have time for anything but the essentials. Each one ends with an Action Step—something you can do today, in less than 20 minutes, to increase your odds of success and make your life better.

At the end of the book, you'll find my favourite resources—podcasts and other books—that will make you better at your business and will also connect you with a community of entrepreneurs around the world who learn from and inspire each other.

You'll also find my email address and social media links, because I'm here for you, too. I'm a huge fan of women "doing it on their own," carving their unique path through life and often inventing their own jobs so they can be there for their families. If you have a question or just need to talk to someone who has been through it before, I'd love to connect.

In the meantime, I encourage you to start making your way through the chapters that follow, whether you want to read right through from start to finish or just set aside an hour each weekend to read one chapter. When you gain skills, life gets easier.

Whatever you do, don't give up on your dream. Your breakthrough moment could be right around the corner.

And I'm right here, waiting to celebrate your success with you. So, grab a notebook (yes, you will need one) and a highlighter to mark this book up. Let's get started on your best you!

part one

STRATEGIES FOR SUCCESS

At every stage of your career, there are certain skills that will take you a long way.

Master them now.

DREAM IT,
SEE IT,
WORK FOR IT,
ACHIEVE IT

> *Mom, I hear of other women achieving amazing things in their lives and careers, and I wonder what I need to do to make that happen for me!*

Too many people hold themselves back from achieving their dreams because they don't believe in themselves, which is so sad! We all have so much potential we aren't using. I believe we're meant to live our lives to the fullest.

The first step is to be crystal clear on your goals and aspirations.

Being clear on what I want, writing it down and creating vision boards have been extremely valuable tools in helping me achieve my goals.

As you know, I am a very visual person and like to be surrounded by images of the things I want to achieve. I talk about my dream board in the goal-setting chapter ahead, but it can be as simple as tacking a few pictures on your wall. For me, the way this works best is to have a concrete goal list illustrated with photos and magazine pictures.

In addition, tell the people around you what it is you are after—explain your dreams to them so they understand what it is you are working toward.

The first time I experienced the power in this approach was when I was in my mid-30s. I'd always had a very basic car, but it had become important to me to drive something nicer. Now I'm in my late 50s, this seems like a strange goal, but hey, it is what I wanted then. I also had three kids, so I cut out a picture of a Volvo station wagon and put it in my diary. A year later, I was promoted to a job that included a $500 monthly car allowance, which allowed me to get that nice car.

I truly believe I was working toward that outcome with each extra hour and effort I put into my job, and those extra hours and efforts were fuelled partly by having the image in front of me every day.

Another time, I really wanted to take you and your sisters to Salt Spring Island and told a few people I was going to try and make it happen in the coming years. I did the research and found it was quite expensive to rent a house there big enough for you girls and your partners. But on a plane to Chicago, I sat beside a gentleman on his way to France who was doing a month-long house exchange—his house on Salt Spring for an apartment in Paris. I asked him if he and his wife would like to visit Vancouver sometime and might consider a house exchange with me. He said it sounded great and, six months later, we made it happen. It was a fantastic experience and didn't cost us a dime.

If you take just one thing away from this book, I hope it is to dream big and expect your dreams to come true for you. Not by magic, but with hard work and serious commitment. This stuff works—so be careful what you wish for!

YOUR ACTION STEP

Social scientists say we make hundreds, even thousands, of small and large decisions each day. Clear goals and a detailed, technicolour vision at the forefront of your mind make those decisions easier and much likelier to move you in the direction you want to go.

Today, just make a quick list of your top three to five goals in each of these categories: family and relationships, career or business, and financial. You can give each more thought as you work through the chapter ahead, but for now, begin to create a space for dreaming in your head and in your life.

Put your list somewhere you'll see it regularly, and let your mind start doing its thing.

GOAL SETTING, THE MASTER'S EDITION

> *Mom, how do I stay focused on my goals? I seem to get pulled off course — a lot.*

I am convinced the reason we get pulled away from our most important tasks is that we lose sight of our ultimate goals. We need to be reminded of those goals, every moment of every day.

I could write an entire book about goal setting, as it is the most fundamental, important set of actions you will take when you create a business. As someone wise once said, "If you are not working towards your dreams and goals, you are most likely working towards someone else's."

9

As mentioned in the last chapter, I am a huge believer in dream boards—putting your goals in a visual form. I was introduced to this idea in a class I took many years ago, and it revolutionized my ability to achieve my goals. An image really is "worth a thousand words," as the adage goes. Now I have all my goals in picture form on the back pages of a planner I use every day.

How well does this work, you ask? I dreamt of a ski house that could comfortably fit my family and your families and had a photo of a mansion on the slopes of a fabulous ski resort. At the time, mind you, I didn't even have an apartment at a ski resort. But 12 years later, we are building our 3,500-square-foot ski-in-ski-out dream home in the second-largest resort in Canada.

I pasted in photos that symbolized spending more time with my family—12 years later, I was able to retire from full-time work to do that, along with writing this book. And yes, you guessed it: there is a picture of a book there as well.

So how do you get started? Of course, the first step is to imagine big. I always start by asking what I'd be doing if money was no object and I had all the time in the world. Then decide where you will put these pictures. The best place is on a bulletin board right in sight. (As I travelled a lot for work, I used my daily planner because it was always with me.) Grab some scissors and a bunch of old magazines, or print some images from Pinterest or Instagram, and get started.

Consider the following categories:

1.   **FAMILY AND RELATIONSHIP GOALS.** It is said that the state of your well-being can be determined by the state of your relationships, which can also affect your productivity. What could you do to strengthen the relationships in your life? Date nights? Grab an image of a couple at dinner or on a night ski together and put it on the wall. Then commit to carving out time for this activity each week. And yes, you guessed it—because it is on the wall right in front of you, you will see it every day, reminding you that you need to put it on your calendar for the week ahead.

2.   **PHYSICAL GOALS.** If your body is a well-oiled machine, you'll perform better in every aspect of your life. Maybe you want to get back into cycling. Grab an image of someone on a bike to remind you to get back out there. Maybe you want to lose a few pounds—put up a photo of you when you felt your best.

3.   **CAREER GOALS.** Here is where you should dream especially big. If your ultimate goal is to grow your company to 100 employees, grab a company photo with lots of people. If your dream is to have your company stay about the size it is right now, but you want to include family members on your team, get some t-shirts made up and have everyone pose for a picture. Always aim for the absolute best result you can imagine.

4.   **FINANCIAL GOALS.** Here is where you can go crazy. Would you like a 50-foot sailboat? (I still have one of these on my board.) Find an image of the best-looking boat you can. Do you want to go helicopter skiing? (Yes, also on my board.) When the comedian and actor Jim Carrey was totally broke, he wrote a cheque to himself for $10 million for "acting services rendered," payable in three years (1995). He spent time every day imagining himself as a successful actor while also working his butt off. (It doesn't work otherwise.) Just before the cheque was about to come due, he received a $10-million contract to star in the movie *Dumb and Dumber*. Remember the sky is the limit here, so think big, and again, be careful what you hope for, because this stuff works!

5.   **MENTAL DEVELOPMENT GOALS.** This is always a big one for me. I need to be forever growing, and it is easier than ever these days. I always set aside time to read books about business, personal development and anything else that might help my business grow. If this interests you as well, see my recommended reading list at the back. Now it is even easier to do this with podcasts, so I've also included a list of the great ones I listen to. I believe that if you are not learning, you are dying!

6. **LAST BUT NOT LEAST ARE YOUR RECREATIONAL AND SOCIAL GOALS.** What fires you up that you don't do enough because you don't have enough time? Many people don't schedule recreation and social time, but it's a huge mistake—nothing is more important for our mental health, resilience and long-term productivity. Fun and spending time with people we care about ignite us, make us creative and help us to be better at our life's work. I love to golf. I am not good at it nor do I need to be good at it; it makes me happy. For many years, I didn't have time, but I started going to a ladies' "nine and dine," (nine holes and dinner). It killed two passions with one activity. I golfed with my good friends, and we shared a meal afterwards. It meant I had to stop work at 4 p.m. those afternoons, but honestly, I think I got more work done, knowing I had to get going, than if I had slogged through to 6 p.m. or even later.

I really cannot say enough about creating a dream board to affirm your goals visually. Spend a few minutes each day looking at your images, and your subconscious will take hold of those goals in ways you can't imagine. You won't be able to keep yourself from moving toward them.

This is also a great way to drown out any negative thoughts that arise with positive ones, improving the quality of your work throughout the day.

YOUR ACTION STEP

Get out your calendar and block a half hour sometime in the next week to start on your dream board. In that 30 minutes, gather your materials (old magazines, a poster board, markers and pencil crayons—whatever you want to play with) and then block another half hour the following week to get started on putting it all together. Do this until you are content that your board captures your dreams and goals.

MAKING A GREAT FIRST IMPRESSION

> *Mom, I'm confused about what I should wear when I'm at the office or when meeting with clients. Sometimes I feel overdressed, but other times I feel like I should have dressed up more. Could you give me some direction?*

Let's face it; this is a real challenge for women in the workplace. It's another topic that really deserves its own book!

It is a confusing time, as the norm is casual in most industries these days. If you work in this kind of relaxed atmosphere, take the lead from those above you rather than those below or beside you. Upper management is watching.

If all they see you wearing is shorts and flip-flops, how will they know you are up to the challenge of representing the company?

When you have a function coming up, whether it's a client meeting or an office party, ask your supervisor or manager what she will be wearing to be clear about the dress code. Let's say you have important people coming into the office for a critical meeting—you definitely don't want to be overdressed or underdressed, so if you're unsure, just ask. I would much rather have someone spend the time to check with me than be unsure of what to wear.

A few key tips for your employees or those who report to you who are new to business:

1. If it is appropriate for a nightclub, it is inappropriate for work, unless you work in a nightclub. (The same is true of the beach and yoga class.)

2. Dress sharp, even if your outfit is casual.

3. Nice shoes are always a good touch, even if you have jeans on. (My dad always spent a lot of money on shoes. He wore a suit every day, but they weren't expensive—it was his shoes he considered investments. We had every single type of shoe-shining contraption on the market, and Sunday afternoons were always shoe-shining time. He spent hours making sure they were perfect.)

4. Spend a bit of money on accessories. Your laptop bag should be expensive even if you can't really afford it! For people who don't know you, this signals the calibre of person with whom they are dealing.

5. Good grooming is also essential. Always be fresh and clean even it if means running to the gym to shower after an all-nighter!!

For most of my career, I worked in the home theatre industry. Our leading products were high-end, expensive custom speakers that were installed in walls and ceilings, and our target market was the wealthy one percent with large disposable incomes. The people we sold to, however, were install-ers—and most could not afford these luxury products. When they came to trade shows to look at all the new gear, they typically wore jeans and t-shirts and were usually not used to dealing with people wearing suits and ties. The company I represented embraced that culture, and our people wore matching t-shirts for most shows.

However, I sold these products internationally, in markets where most of my customers were product distributors who always wore a suit and tie. My boss wanted me to wear the "company uniform" (a t-shirt) to a trade show, and I argued the point, saying it would not be seen as professional by our international customers. I lost the battle and ended up wearing the t-shirt. It was the most difficult show I ever worked, and I had already done the job for more than 10 years at that point. My European, Asian and Middle Eastern customers just didn't understand. When I went to visit them or attended shows in their markets, I was always very professionally dressed, which to them signalled that I represented a prestigious company and I respected them and their businesses. My boss came down on the side of looking like a unified team, but our international customers were confused, and their confidence in our company was undermined. In the end, my boss came to understand, and at all shows after that event, my international sales team and I were allowed to wear the clothing we felt was appropriate.

You're right that dress is important. To make the right impression, assessing what you should wear is as important as planning what you will discuss. Rightly or wrongly, people can be quite judgmental about how you present yourself. For their comfort and your confidence level, it is best to stay as neutral and respectful as possible.

I am a big fan of power clothes, pieces you know you look great in when you wear them. It cost me a bit of money, but for every important trip, trade show or meeting, I always invested in something that made me feel special and powerful. It was a huge boost to my ego and set my mood for the event. This doesn't always mean you need to buy something special—but when something important is coming up, give some careful thought to what you'll wear, and make sure you feel special in it.

YOUR ACTION STEP

The women of France are well known for their elegance and fashion sense. Their secret? A few good pieces they wear over and over with different accessories to keep their look from getting stale.

Right now, or as soon as you get home, go to your closet and dig out the outfit you feel best in when you wear it to a business event. Lay it on your bed along with your favourite matching accessories and shoes or boots. Take a photo. Now when you have a big day or feel the need for a pick-me-up, you know what to wear.

Think about what makes this outfit so right for you. Is it comfort, quality, fit, fabric, colour—or a combination of all the above? Write down those details in a note on your smartphone and refer to it anytime you shop.

For extra credit, swap out your first-choice accessories for alternatives to create a second outfit.

ROCKING THAT PRESENTATION

Mom, I have a big presentation coming up, and I'm so anxious.
How can I make sure I do a great job?

"I think it's healthy for a person to be nervous. It means you care—
that you work hard and want to give a great performance.
You just have to channel that nervous energy into the show."

BEYONCÉ KNOWLES
Singer, Songwriter, Business Mogul

Isn't that a great quote?

Use your pre-presentation anxiety as energy and motivation to help you prepare, prepare, prepare! It can help to think of it as "good stress."

I have presented all over the world, to small groups and large crowds. Not surprisingly, my best presentations were those where I knew my material inside and out—the worst were when I thought I could fake it.

Take these easy steps to ensure your best performance:

1. Is your subject technical? If so, are you prepared for the presentation and the questions that may be asked afterwards? If not, prepare more or find someone to help.

2. Decide if you will use any aids, such as PowerPoint, to help you present. If you do, don't read from your slides—know your material so you can just use them as a guide. And do not put too much text on the slides—you will lose people's attention because they think they should be reading.

3. Have at least one knowledgeable person review your material to make sure it is rock solid and 100 percent accurate. If people can poke holes in your presentation, they will.

4. Practise with the material until you could do it in your sleep, and know your timing, including exactly how long it takes from start to finish. If possible, present it to someone. Some of the best presentations I've done were the last couple of stops on a two-week road trip with multiple events. I was so familiar with my material it was second nature and flowed easily.

5. Be sure the room is ready with everything you will need at least an hour in advance. There is nothing worse than scrambling with power cords and microphones as people find their seats—except a late start due to poor communication on the set-up. Starting late signals a lack of respect for your audience's time and makes it a lot harder for you to gain their trust and hold their interest.

6. Make sure your introduction is about you, with a short explanation about why you are there and where you are from, as well as your qualifications to speak on your topic. One of the best presenters I know plays a short video of his accomplishments at the start of each event, so everyone knows who he is. It is really effective.

7. Make sure you let your audience know what you will be doing and how long it will take. Thank them in advance for their time.

8. Start with something humorous about you. The evening before I spoke to 150 people in Sydney, Australia, I showed some of the conference attendees some great photos of me with kangaroos on a golf course. They all humoured me and said something like, "Yes, Linda, great!" By the next morning, however, I'd realized it was like showing Canadians a picture of a squirrel (there are no squirrels in Australia), so I shared my thought with the crowd. It got them laughing and lightened the mood.

9. This is critical: remember that 98 percent of the people in the room could not get up and speak in front of a crowd. When someone reminded me of this, it gave me added confidence. I also find it helpful to use affirmations like, "I am the best at presenting this information," or, "I know people will learn something and feel this is a great use of their time."

10. Move around throughout the presentation and make eye contact with many people in the audience. Even in these days of Twitter updates and short attention spans, it is much harder to lose them if they know you are watching.

11. Know your audience and dress appropriately. If you know everyone will be in jeans, wear business casual rather than conservative attire that makes you look like you do not belong. If you know they will all be in suits, wear your best one.

12. Get lots of sleep and don't drink too much coffee! (Sometimes even one cup can be too many when the adrenaline kicks in, and it will.)

13. Slow down! I am sure you have noticed that people tend to rush when they're speaking to an audience. Nerves will do that to you. I like to have a bottle of water and take a sip now and then, as it forces me to slow down and breathe.

14. Start and end on time, leaving a few minutes for questions.

15. This is the hardest part, but I truly feel it is important if you want to be a great presenter: ask for feedback.

16. This time, I've saved the most useful advice for last: take a Dale Carnegie course if you can. If you can't, at least read some of his books, especially *How to Develop Self-Confidence and Influence People by Public Speaking*.

Remember my favourite Dale Carnegie quote: "You can conquer almost any fear if you will only make up your mind to do so. So, remember, fear doesn't exist anywhere except in the mind."

There is no better feeling than when you have truly rocked a presentation. Follow these tips, and you will be well on your way.

YOUR ACTION STEP

This is going to feel silly, but I promise it will serve you well. Stand in front of a mirror, look into your eyes and smile warmly. Do it for long enough to take a full, deep breath.

Start doing it every morning before you brush your teeth.

You're practising "the pause," the masterstroke of accomplished speakers. Next time you're in front of an audience, even if it is coworkers to whom you're presenting a budget, take a moment to make eye contact with a few people. Smile. Focus on making a real connection. With your eyes, let them know you're happy they're there while you take a deep, slow breath.

You've just slowed your heart rate, which will slow your speaking rate—and you've communicated your personal warmth and confidence while connecting with your audience.

REACHING THE TOP 1% OF YOUR FIELD

> *Mom, how can I be sure I'm on my way to becoming the best in my industry?*

> "Run toward the thing that everyone else is running from."
>
> DARREN HARDY
> Author and Speaker

We all know that you will need to embrace fear and suffering to become the best in your field.

Wait, you didn't know that? Yes, I'm afraid the road to success is riddled with obstacles. That's why not everyone is on it. Don't decide what to do with your life based on the rewards you imagine. Think instead about what you'll be willing to do even when it's hard, even when the money isn't coming in, even when you're exhausted and there are still hours of work ahead.

What people often don't realize is that it takes extra effort—an extra 10 percent or so of sweat equity—to be a top one-percenter. Most people will not put in unnecessary effort, and when things get tough, they will give up. They won't take the stairs instead of the elevator. Every time you think of doing something at 90 percent of your best or tell yourself a new challenge is impossible, ask yourself what road you're on. What could you learn by taking the stairs?

If you head for the top, the obstacles you'll experience will seem overwhelming at times. They'll often make you want to quit, to agree with the negative voice in your head that says you aren't good enough.

When that happens, revisit your dream board to remind yourself why you're doing what you're doing. Then revisit this round-up of strategies that can help take you to the top.

1. Know your competition. Who is in the top one percent in your industry today? For most of the 17 years I travelled the world in international sales, I worked for a manufacturer. When I decided to open my agency, I first had to take a close look at the competition. Who was the best at what they did? How did they do it?

2. Identify the factors that will set you apart from the rest. With the ease of digital marketing and speaking to potential customers on Skype, many of the people in my industry chose to do their jobs mainly from a computer in their home. But from travelling, I knew that many people like to buy from people who get to know them and who learn about and appreciate their markets. In my field, understanding the differences between markets and clients was a critical element in achieving success. I knew I needed to budget a lot of time and money for travel to be at the top of my field.

3. Identify your pain threshold for investment in time and money for your new venture. If you want something bad enough, you will do whatever it takes to have it. If you don't, you won't. There is a Chinese proverb that says, "The temptation to give up is the greatest right before you're about to succeed." Are you ready to push past that point? Are you ready to give up time with family and friends? To take risks and possibly even admit to the odd failure along the way? If so, you have what it takes to get to the top.

4. Your goals must be front and centre in your everyday life. Each thought and action must be congruent with your vision. Sounds hard, right? It is. The people in the top one percent never land there by accident. They carefully planned their path and made adjustments to it as they went along. (I talked about this in the goal-setting chapter, but it is worth mentioning here that your success plan can and should be modified from time to time.)

5. You may get the impression you need to work 24/7 to get to the top one percent. But like a professional athlete at the top of her sport, you also need to schedule rest. For me, recovering from work is spending time with family, fitness, writing in my journal, reading, listening to music and fixing and enjoying great food—in no particular order.

6. Know your rhythms and leverage your energy. The morning is the most productive time for me; I am the least productive from about two to four in the afternoon. During those hours, I do routine things, play with my grandchildren, or go for a run, walk or bike ride. Without scheduled breaks in your work, you will not perform at your peak.

YOUR ACTION STEP

Grab your notebook and list the top five competitors in your field. If you don't know, google. Now draw a line down the page and list their primary competitive advantages. For example, these may include size, history, brand recognition, international presence, deep pockets and a stellar reputation as an employer.

If your field is a new one—you've created something unique—consider the companies who might adapt your service or product to make it their own if it becomes successful (as Apple did to BlackBerry, for instance).

Now, take another page, and write down the five competitive characteristics of You Inc.* someone doing this exercise in five years might identify about your organization.

Yes, that's you or your business.

WHEN GIVERS
MEET TAKERS

Mom, how do I know when enough is enough when it comes to helping others?

"The more credit you give away, the more will come back to you. The more you help others, the more they will want to help you."

BRIAN TRACY,
Personal Development Author, Motivational Speaker

"You can get everything in life you want if you will just help enough other people get what they want."

ZIG ZIGLAR,
Author, Salesman, Motivational Speaker

This is a big topic for me. Now that I'm in my late 50s, I can say for sure that giving back is something you will never regret. As you can see from the quotes above, it's a belief shared by many successful people. But there are some situations—with a particular type of person—where you'll need to protect yourself and your generosity.

When I was in my 30s, when we were building a new house and I was completing the third year of my MBA while caring for three kids under six and managing a full-time job, I did not understand the concept of giving back. Quite honestly, I did not live this way. I didn't have time to go to the bathroom let alone give something up to do something for someone else.

Your sister Jackie was four, and she loved her dance class, but I didn't know how I was going to fit it in. She was already a bit lost in the mix, as she'd been the baby until her new sister had recently arrived. I was desperate to make this happen for her but finding the time to drop her off and pick her up was not something I felt I could take on. I voiced this to another mom after picking Jackie up at preschool and the mom said, "I'll do it." She had five kids! Her youngest was in Jackie's class, and her daughter was Jackie's best friend. She said she was interested in enrolling her daughter as well and would be happy to do all the driving to make it happen. It was a good 15 minutes out of her way, each way. Before accepting her offer, I said, "I don't know how I can reciprocate. I am stretched to the limit."

She said, "Please, don't worry. Others have done this type of thing for me in the past. I know you well enough to know that, when things get easier for you, you will pay it forward." (This happened long before "pay it forward" became a thing.)

I was so grateful. And I've told this story many times, as it was a real lesson for me. As she predicted, I have been able to repay this debt to many, many others as the years went by. Today I feel like I have not only repaid her kindness and generosity but have a lot in the bank.

That said, it's important to remember that not all people are givers. Adam Grant wrote one of the best books of 2013, *Give and Take*, in which he categorizes three types of traits in business people: givers, takers and matchers.

Matchers are people who try to give and take equally, always trying to make sure the transaction is fair. Givers give, but they're prone to burnout and possible exploitation. Takers take: they're the ones always looking to offload tasks, leave early or get out of almost anything. Sometimes they are hard to identify at first, but the signs are always there. They are usually take-charge personality types, so you are likely to be initially deceived into thinking they are working hard. Once you identify a taker, strategically protect your time and energy.

When under pressure from a taker, use responses like:

1. *"I would love to help, but I am working on an important project that needs to be completed by Monday. Give me a call then." Takers are often impatient and will find some other sucker before Monday.*

2. *If you are in a corporate environment, try "I will check with my boss to make sure she is okay with me spending time on that. We have a lot going on right now."*

3. *"Have you asked Sally?" (Make sure Sally is the type who never falls for takers.) "She is quite good at that, and she may not be in the middle of anything. I'm afraid I am."*

4. *"Interesting—we should get a committee together" is always a good one, as takers like immediate action, not deliberation.*

Givers are some of the most successful people, going on to achieve extraordinary results in many industries. Don't give up giving—just make sure you are managing it in a way that aligns with your goals.

YOUR ACTION STEP

Grab your notebook. Think back: when was the last time you said yes when you meant no, or said yes and regretted it later?

Give yourself a do-over. Play that conversation through in your head, and then write a response to the person who asked.

Make your answer firm and gracious. For example, "I'm grateful you thought of me, but I'm afraid my plate is full these days." Or, "I'm looking forward to taking on new things when I get current with my schedule—until then, my calendar is full." Find something that feels comfortable for you to say, even if it takes 10 tries. Believe me, this investment in time will pay off a thousand-fold or more.

Once you've hit on phrasing that feels right for you, repeat it aloud five times. Then write it on a business card and put it in your wallet. Each time you're asked to take on something new, remember it's there and available to you as an option.

EXTRA CREDIT: remember that every yes is a no to something else in your life—there is no such thing as "extra time." Only you can protect your dreams.

GIVE, GIVE AND GIVE SOME MORE

Mom, I think I get the giving back thing. But sometimes it's so hard when I feel like I am just getting by paycheque to paycheque myself.

"It is one of the beautiful compensations in this life that no one can sincerely try to help another without helping themselves."

RALPH WALDO EMERSON
American Poet, Essayist, Visionary

"It is literally true that you can succeed best and quickest by helping others to succeed."

NAPOLEON HILL
Author of *Think and Grow Rich*

I know you've heard about giving back from me all your life, and I touch on the subject elsewhere in this book. But I believe in it so much I wanted to devote an entire chapter to it. Articles, books and speeches by successful people invariably include something about giving and the impact it has on what you get back. This is not a new concept—as you can see above, the man often referred to as the father of self-help, Napoleon Hill, talked about it in the early 1900s.

The theory is simple. When you offer what you have to help someone else, they are always looking for ways to repay you. You may be saying, "Well, that doesn't seem genuine." But there is a feeling of pure joy when you can give something to someone, and the recipient will also open up to try to help someone else. They'll see how great it was for them to be on the receiving end of kindness, and they will want to pass it on. (Not everyone, obviously, but most people.) When you're feeling fearful about money, helping someone less fortunate can help put things in perspective and make you feel better.

You know how you feel when you have purchased the perfect present for someone? Something you know they need and want and is perfect for the occasion? You can't wait for them to open it! The joy you feel at that moment is the "giving high" humans experience when we're fortunate enough to be able to give to or do something kind for someone else. It doesn't have to be huge—giving up your seat on the bus to someone who looks tired can change the quality of your whole day for the better. (And theirs!)

Everyone has had this feeling sometimes, I am sure, but it isn't always easy to remember.

In a blog post for *Scientific American*, author, MacArthur Fellow and psychologist Maria Konnikova wrote:

"Not only is the gift recipient likely to be appreciative, but we ourselves may benefit. Generosity—which in this definition actually includes generosity of time and generosity that is both unexpected and spontaneous (in stark contrast to the list-variety of the present)—is one of the top three predictors of a successful marriage, a surprising addition to the expected culprits, sexual intimacy and commitment. It can make us feel better about ourselves. It can help us actually be happier and see the world as an overall better place."

Our generosity convinces us that the world is full of opportunity; life returns our generosity to us in full measure and then some. And when we feel better, we do better. This is not to say you should always look to receive when you give. That isn't how it works—that isn't giving, it's trading. But those who try to live with open hands and hearts learn quickly that we're bound to receive more than we give.

Try it. When it's hard, try harder.

I guarantee you will not be disappointed!

YOUR ACTION STEP

Thank someone for their contribution to your life today. You can do it by email, post, telephone or even on social media. But try to write at least three detailed sentences making it clear what it is you are thanking them for. For example, no "Thank you for being my sister." Instead, try something like, "Thank you for always being at my soccer games, even when it was pouring, and for always making me feel like you were my biggest fan. Thank you for helping me convince Mom to let me quit soccer to take up hip-hop. And thank you for your laugh, which makes me happy every time I hear it."

PASSION, THE FUEL OF CHAMPIONS

Mom, how do I find my passion?

Have you ever had a restaurant server who believed so much in what she was selling that you ordered it even though you didn't think you wanted it? (You may have even thought to yourself, "Wow, could I ever use this person in my organization!") These remarkable servers usually suggest what they love to eat or drink themselves and so are passionate about their recommendations. This is real marketing. As simple as it sounds, this is how you become a great salesperson—by developing the power to convince someone to purchase something they may have no idea they need—but that you know will make their life better or easier.

Find passion for your product or service, and you will achieve greatness.

The dictionary says passion is "a strong emotion, an ardent love; zeal; eager desire, hope and joy."

Think of the most celebrated people you know, the ones who have reached the top of their field. A passion for giving it their all, for being the best they can be, is something they all have in common. People may become successful without this kind of passion, but their success or the pleasure they feel about their success will not last. Passion fuels creativity and ignites energy in everything you do.

American motivational speaker, life coach and author Gabrielle Bernstein once said, "Allow your passion to become your purpose, and it will one day become your profession." How do you find your passion? What would make you jump out of bed each morning and work 12 to 15 hours? Because this is the kind of energy, enthusiasm, determination and commitment you'll need to be great at what you do!

Willpower won't do it; self-discipline won't do it (although it will help to bridge some inevitable energy gaps). Passion is the only fuel that burns hot, steady and long enough to build a truly successful career.

YOUR ACTION STEP

Get out your notebook and draw a line down the middle of a page.

On one side, make a list of everything you've ever done that energized you and made you lose track of time. (Building a tree house? Reading? Running? Planning a new project with friends or colleagues?)

On the other, make a list of everything you've done in the last year that drained your energy.

Don't make it too hard. You're just getting some insight into the kinds of activities that light you up and the ones that drain your light.

MASTERING YOUR TIME

part two

There is only one thing in life that is truly limited—the number of hours we're given in a lifetime.

Learning to use your time effectively is an essential part of achieving the life you want.

EAT THAT FROG

> *Mom, how do I get the big things done?*
> *My goals always feel so overwhelming!*

Brian Tracy, another of my mentors, has done a great deal of teaching on time management. One of the things that really helped me was his insistence that the last 15 minutes of each day should be set aside for planning the next day. Mornings are much easier when you start with a fresh list that begins with your toughest projects and includes them all, no matter how small. Don't forget to add personal to-dos, as they also take time and need to be scheduled.

Taking this time at the end of the day is important because, more often than not, your morning will otherwise start with fires that need putting out. The next thing you know it is lunch, and you still haven't made your list!

Brian also tells us that the easiest way to leverage your day is to "eat that frog." In other words, take the toughest task on your list and do it first. (It's often the thing you have procrastinated on for days or even weeks. Yes, that one.) Doing this gives you great momentum for getting other things on the list done. Try it! I swear by this strategy because it works so well.

I am a huge fan of using a daily planner, the old-fashioned paper kind. In my experience, it helps focus. You can't be tempted by the ding of a new text if you're not near your computer or phone. My favourite is the week-at-a-glance kind with a section for a list of to-dos. There is something psycho-logically rewarding and motivating about checking off a bunch of tasks on a page and seeing those checkmarks throughout the day.

PRO TIP: If you move a task ahead to the next day or next week, put it in a different colour or number it, so you are aware of how many times you have put it off. If you keep putting it off, ask yourself if it needs to be done at all. If not, cross it off your list. If it does, are you the best person to do it? It may be that this is something you should delegate. Either way, do it or pass it on. Reclaim the energy it took to carry the mental obligation around.

Are you having trouble with a project? Is putting it off getting you into trouble or causing you needless stress? Maybe you need to be honest with whoever is expecting you to get the job done and explain why you are having trouble. They may be able to offer some advice to help get you started.

You may also find starting is the hardest part; once you do, it just flows. As a lifelong runner, I often go out when it is cold and dark—or when I'd just rather not. I read in a running magazine that you should commit to running for just 10 minutes. More often than not, the first 10 minutes is the hard-est—once you get out there, you find it is okay to keep going.

This is often the case with a large project you really don't want to do, too. Once you start, it isn't long before you settle into a rhythm. Next thing you know, it turns out not to be the frog you thought it was.

YOUR ACTION STEP

Go through your calendar for the last two weeks and identify your frogs. Of each day, ask yourself if there was something that felt like it was hanging over your head. Think about how it affected your energy and how you would have felt if you'd done it first thing.

STAYING ON TRACK

Mom, I can't seem to get my to-do list done. My days get away from me!

We all have those days, and those of us who take on way more than we can do (which describes most of us entrepreneurs) are also the ones who tend to get derailed most easily. Everything's urgent, am I right? But as *7 Habits of Highly Effective People* author Stephen Covey taught, not everything is important. I am a big fan of figuring out what is important and what is "just urgent" as the day unfolds. Take the extra second to analyze everything that crosses your desk—how essential is this task in moving you forward on today's most important accomplishments?

Before we go on, I'm assuming you've read the chapters on goal setting and time management ("Eat That Frog") and have made your to-do list. At the end of the day yesterday, you invested 15 minutes to plan today, to make sure you are focused on the most important things on your list, the ones required to take you toward your goals.

If not, do that first and then come back.

Now ...

1. Set aside some quiet time for the must-dos on your list. Put this time on your calendar. Just as you wouldn't miss a meeting with an important client because something came up, you should commit fully to this time with yourself and make it your first priority. For many years, my strategy was to start work before anyone else to create some time when the rest of the world did not know I was working. I often got much of my entire day's work done before the day technically even started. It also energized me—I felt like I could take on the world. Try it.

2. Identify the hardest thing on your list, the one you may be procrastinating on, and put it on your calendar today. Now do it. Again, no excuses. Once you can mark this one done, you will be amazed at how the rest of your list gets easier.

3. Don't be afraid to say no. If you are always getting derailed, there may be a reason for it. You may have a target on your back—everyone knows you can be counted on to take on anything that needs doing. If so, you may be attracting people who will take advantage of your good nature.

4. Don't be afraid to delegate a task to someone who has more time or skill or who may just be in a better position to take it on. Look at each item on your list each night and ask yourself if you are the best person to be doing it.

5. Turn off your phone, Skype, Messenger and any other way people reach you for at least an hour each day. Don't be afraid—if you were in a meeting, you would be unreachable. Isn't productive time equally important?

6. Create an email schedule. Deal with your inbox in the morning and then again later in the day, but whatever you do, don't respond to emails as they arrive. We can often get caught up with instant message modes of communication and end up glued to it all day long. If necessary, set up an auto-responder suggesting that emailers call you (or even better, your assistant) if their matter is urgent.

7. In every office, there is usually at least one person who just likes to chat, someone who will occupy lots of your attention if allowed, without any productive outcome. You may need to find a polite way to let this person know you just don't have time.

Most importantly, look back at your day and work out how successful or unsuccessful you were at meeting your goals for the day. This is particularly important if you feel you lose control of your day every day. I used to have a fantastic sales manager who was regularly pulled into other people's projects because he was so good at them. As he was under my direction, I would often speak with him at the end of the day and ask him how his day went, and he'd tell me he was helping the graphics team with the website corrections or some other non-sales activity. As we were only paid if we sold something, I finally made him put a sticky note on his laptop that asked, "Is what I am doing making me money?" He said it helped him focus on what was important and necessary to achieve his goals—and to avoid getting sidetracked with the goals of others.

Mark Zuckerberg said, "The question I ask myself almost every day is, 'Am I doing the most important thing I could be doing?'" I encourage you to ask yourself the same question even more often.

YOUR ACTION STEP

Decide right now when you will check and deal with your email each day. If necessary, set up an auto-responder to let people know when you will get back to them and give them an option for urgent matters. (If you don't know how to do this, google.)

Now decide which hours of the day you're going to be offline to focus on commitments you've already made.

THE PERNICIOUS
MYTH OF
MULTITASKING

> *Mom, I can't seem to get as much done as I used to. I feel like I could do several things at once before — now I can't concentrate!*

My entire working life, I was convinced I was a super multitasker. This convenient fiction was drilled into me from all over. As the mother of three children and a business owner, I was expected to make it all work, all at the same time.

What I have since realized is that the brain is not made to function this way. Of course, computers can multitask—but here is what happens when humans try:

1. One study showed that multitasking caused as much as a 15-point drop in IQ on any given task

2. Switching back and forth between tasks can consume as much as 40 percent of productive time.

3. You are more likely to lose focus when you are working on more than one thing—you are more easily distracted.

4. Habitual multitaskers are not able to focus even when they are not multitasking, as they are more often and easily distracted.

5. It is more difficult to retain information when multitasking, so you learn and remember less.

So how do we resist the urge to try to multitask, especially when we have a never-ending to-do list?

1. Focus on one task at a time and allow yourself a certain amount of time to finish it. (Be realistic—don't create unnecessary stress by underestimating the amount of time a task will take.)

2. Set an alarm to let you know when you reach the end of the allotted time, so you don't need to watch the clock.

3. Put your phone on airplane mode to avoid being distracted by calls, emails or social media.

4. Take regular breaks. It may seem counterintuitive but taking a five-minute break to get some water or walk around your office can spur you on to finish the task strong. (Just don't stay at your desk and check Facebook—you need to move.)

If you are allowed to focus on one task without any distractions, you can save a lot of time and make your work time much more productive.

Stress also plays a factor in productivity. The more stress we're managing, the harder it is to concentrate, making simple tasks more difficult to finish. It reminds me of a hamster on a wheel: the wheel goes faster and faster as you continue to add more things to your ever-growing to-do list. The list grows longer, your stress level goes up and it becomes harder to concentrate, making your list grow longer.

My solution to this is to back away from the office. Increase your productivity by taking a break and going to your happy place to reconnect with yourself.

In my case, it is a walk, run, cycle or ski—any activity that takes me into nature. I can get lost in it, which creates a different frame of reference and makes me remember that life is about more than the to-do list.

You will have your own happy place, but the important thing is to find it. It tells your brain you are now safe, far away from the stress creators. You will be much more effective when you get back to work—your focus will be sharper, and your list will shrink much faster.

YOUR ACTION STEP

This may be the most important question you ask yourself all year: Am I scheduling more than it is possible to do within the physical reality of time?

If so, you're very likely to be moving through each day feeling both rushed and behind. You may not even notice it anymore, but the stress created by that feeling is diminishing your focus, creativity and ability to be present to the people you love. It may be affecting the quality of your sleep, mood and long-term health.

Rushing through life doesn't make us faster. It makes us more anxious and less effective.

If this question resonates with you, schedule a half hour on your calendar this week to take the next step: identifying those things in your week you can let go of. Think of this as a non-negotiable—you will never, ever beat the laws of physics, but you may be able to give up your volunteer gig for now or pay someone else to do the laundry.

part three

THE EMPLOYED
ENTREPRENEUR

Entrepreneurial skills aren't just essential for business owners and the self-employed.

In today's rapidly shifting work culture, they'll help you advance and achieve your personal and career goals.

GETTING THE PROMOTION YOU DESERVE

> *Mom, I am trying to get ahead but it seems others get noticed and promoted before me. How do I turn this around?*

When Dwayne "The Rock" Johnson was interviewed for Fortune magazine, he said he was often asked about the "secret to success."

No wonder—after being evicted from their apartment because his mom couldn't pay the rent (when he was 15), he decided he'd never be in a similar position again. He went on to become a hugely successful wrestler, breaking stadium attendance records, and then a top-grossing film star known for his social media marketing savvy and 57 million followers.

His reply? "There is no secret. Be humble, be hungry and always be the hardest worker in the room."

Many a great job was obtained with this philosophy.

My dad (or as I sometimes refer to him, my "sales-genius father, Roger") gave me another valuable lesson. He taught me to always be the first to arrive, even if it meant standing on a cold sidewalk until the person with the key got there. He also taught me to take enthusiasm and passion into every project—no one wants a doubter on the team, so always look at the positives and be encouraging at all times.

Zig Ziglar, a well-known speaker who has written more than 33 books on business, said: "The way you see life will largely determine what you get out of it." Lots can be said about this, but in brief, be the person you want to hang out with—the happy, positive, glass-half-full kind of person everyone wants on their team.

Always be punctual with deadlines and show a willingness to complete projects on time. Don't be afraid to let your supervisor or manager know if there is a snag. Unavoidable events may cause project delays, so make sure you tell your manager why you are delayed and what the consequences are. Be upfront at all times. Your boss is likely committed to a deadline with her boss, and if you blindside her with a "Sorry, I tried my best" when the project is due, you will not make her look good. It is better to give progress reports, even if she doesn't seem to care. She can see how far you have progressed or, in the case of delays, be aware of the likelihood of missed deadlines and make appropriate judgments about how to handle upline reporting. (I know you don't need to be reminded of this, but people who can't be counted on all the time can't be counted on *ever*, and that's the kiss of death to a promising career. People who can be counted on are surprisingly rare, and because you are one of those people, you will go far.)

Whatever you do, do not assume you understand what your boss is dealing with. As the famous saying goes, ASSUMING only makes an "ass out of you and me"! This is something for which you do not want to be responsible.

You may wonder what your work at your current job has to do with getting your next job, but the truth is, nothing could be more important. The world is small, and most interviews—even those outside your current employer—are not cold calls but opportunities that arise because someone who enjoyed working with you as a boss, colleague, customer or even competitor heard about the opportunity and thought of you. (Because you're great.)

Here are a few other strategies to think about:

1. When aiming for a new position, work through any fear and doubt—during the interview, you must at all times feel 100 percent sure you are the best person for the job. In the working-through phase, remember that no one would be "perfect" for the job. If you are willing to work the hardest, then you are absolutely the best person.

2. When interviewing, don't ever make anyone think this isn't the dream job you have been waiting for. In other words, if this is a stepping stone to other places you want to go, don't make your ambition part of your pitch to get the job. The person making the decision may feel it is an extremely important job, and you don't want to make it seem like you would not be forever grateful to have it.

3. Be confident, but not arrogant. There is a huge difference. In an interview, confidently explain how you feel your skills are the best for the position. Be careful you don't criticize what has been done in the past—the person interviewing you may have had the job or supervised someone who did. Instead, let them know you can enhance future outcomes with your experience and skills.

4. Be overly prepared for all interviews. Create your own questions about the position. Sit down and write out the skills that make you stand out.

Above all, express gratitude for the opportunity. If you do not get the job, follow up to ask why so you can incorporate what you learn into your next interview. (Don't assume you know why, as your assumptions will likely be wrong.)

YOUR ACTION STEP

Go through the list on the previous page and number the items according to their relevance to you. Which is the most likely to give you trouble? The next most likely to be especially hard for you?

Now, write a quick list of things you can do to help you with your number one challenge. Do you have a friend or mentor who is great at talking you through these things? Is there a TED talk or class addressing the skills you need to strengthen? Will writing about your fears help you see them more clearly and overcome them? Is there someone you admire who has faced similar challenges and would be willing to share advice?

SURVIVING A BAD BOSS

> Mom, I can't stand my boss anymore!
> He undermines me, doesn't give me the
> information or support I need to do my job,
> and then takes credit for my accomplishments.
> What do I do?

Remember that these things happen; they will be harmful only if you let them. As we all know, everyone is dealing with a different set of experiences. We may also be dealing with something that makes it difficult to look the situation objectively.

Whatever you do, don't take it personally. Women tend to do this, and it only makes matters worse.

Does your boss feel threatened by you? Do you get the impression he feels you are too eager, too connected or just too good at your job?

It seems completely unfair, I know, but you have to realize there will always be people who are promoted above their abilities and who therefore feel terribly insecure. They may have done a great job in some other capacity for the company; eventually, there was no choice but to promote them. Sometimes, companies unwisely give promotions because they can't afford much of a pay raise. The promotion might even be a favour done for a friend or one of those situations in which higher-ups didn't have time to do a proper search and so slid in the most convenient option. The result could be that your boss ended up in a position for which he is not qualified. When this happens, usually everyone knows it, including him!

So, what do you do about this situation? Do you moan to everyone who will listen, or take action?

If you want to make this work—if there is no way around this person who holds your fate in his hands—you may need to suck it up and find out how to help him. What is it that makes him inadequate at the job? Are you able to help him achieve the success he needs to hang on? Or is it a hopeless situation?

Be very careful at this point, as it is easy to make several errors. If you support him too well, you could make him look too good. You will then be stuck in this position forever, as he may not give you any credit at all, meaning you'll be passed over for other, better roles. Whatever you do, remember you may be creating a great friend or a formidable foe, especially if this person does have inside connections.

Above all, again, don't let it become personal. Many people let this type of thing consume them, affecting their work, their personal lives and even their health.

REPEAT AFTER ME: this is only temporary. Don't let it make you a bitter person.

YOUR ACTION STEP

In your notebook, write this down:

Having a bad boss makes me stronger.

Now, spend 10 minutes writing down the reasons this is true, even if the only thing you can come up with is the fact you've now experienced what it is like to work for a bad boss, so you can be a better boss yourself.

part four

STRENGTHENING YOUR PEOPLE POWER

Wherever you are, wherever you go, your ability to lead and collaborate with others will determine how well you do.

AM I TURNING INTO A BITCH?

> Mom, a colleague told me someone on my team is calling me a bitch. I know some people don't like me because of my position. What's the best way to deal with this?

How often do we hear some variation of, "Sure, she is successful—but that's because she is a bitch"? Accomplished women still can't catch a break on this one.

When women rise to the top of their fields, some people will assume they climbed there by stepping on others all the way up.

There is no question hard decisions often need to be made. Some of those decisions will mean other people get hurt, and those people may strike back. There is a reason "it's not personal; it's business" has been said many, many times.

The important thing to remember is that you were hired to do a job, which includes making decisions that are in line with the company's goals. One of the hardest parts of any responsible role is knowing your decisions may not always make life better for the people around you.

You are not there to make friends. Being friends with those you work with—not friendly, which is essential, but close friends—may end up hurting at least one of you. For example, I worked with a friend for 15 years, a gentleman I'll call David. We met while working at different companies in the same field; when I started my own company, I hired him. He worked in a sales role, and there were several times in our working relationship that some difficult decisions had to be made. This may have gone terribly wrong and our friendship could have been lost. Because it was my own company, I had the luxury of taking David aside each time to explain the big picture and let him know why I had to make the decisions I did. If it isn't your own company, you may not be free to do this—sometimes, managers and executives simply have to take the brunt of their employees' hurt and anger because they aren't free to share the bigger-picture strategies.

In hindsight, it was a great lesson. When people are armed with all the facts surrounding a decision, they are more often able to understand it. Let's face it: misunderstandings are mostly due to a lack of information. How often do you get upset about a situation, only to find out you didn't have all the details? When we understand why choices have to be made, we're more likely to stay fully engaged and supportive of our company's goals and leadership. So, when hard or unpopular decisions are unavoidable, share as much information as possible with the people affected. At the very least, they'll appreciate your efforts and concern.

I had a boss early on in my career who said, "Business is not difficult. It is people who make it hard."

Three out of every four employees say that dealing with their boss is the worst and most stressful part of their job. Fully 65 percent of employees say they would rather have a different boss than a pay raise! (Wow, that is huge.) Some of this resentment is inevitable: most of us don't like being told what to do or to have someone watching over us. However, in the majority of organizations, this is still the way things work.

My point in telling you this story is that you can eliminate some of the negative feelings others will otherwise experience by being honest and upfront. But you may also find some people jump to conclusions easily and are stubborn about letting them go, even when those conclusions are proven incorrect.

I've realized over the years that those who called me a bitch (or something along those lines) didn't know me and didn't take the time to find out who I really am.

Here is the most important thing I'd like you to remember on this topic: as women, we like to be liked, but business is not a popularity contest. If we want to be successful, we usually have to look elsewhere for warmth and friendship.

YOUR ACTION STEP

Here is another potentially life-changing question to ask yourself: Do I believe other people have an obligation to like me?

If this feels true for you, make a quick list of people you simply haven't warmed to in recent memory, perhaps because they reminded you of someone in your past who was problematic, because they have different values or beliefs, or because they just weren't your jam. Some people love Paul McCartney and some love Ringo Starr. (And some people can't remember the names of any of the Beatles and just don't care!) Some people will love you, and some people won't. And that's okay, as long as you love you.

FIREPROOFING YOUR BRIDGES

> *Mom, there is a person in my department who is driving me crazy. I don't see how I can work with him.*

As we have talked about many times, your success at work depends on impressing your supervisors and doing everything you can to further their goals. It can be much harder to do when someone on your team isn't pulling his weight. Be mindful, though, that the people who work beside or under you in terms of seniority today may be very important to you at some point in the future.

In the middle of my career, I was hired to be a senior manager in a start-up. It was an exciting opportunity—I was in my early 30s and managed a cross-country team of 20 people. The start-up was financed by someone I'll call William, a very successful man who had agreed to invest millions in seed money if we hired his son, Billy. Billy had recently graduated from university with a degree in engineering. We were a distribution company and didn't need the services of an engineer, so it was all a bit difficult.

Some important context: we were a small, lean team and most of the employees had taken a pay cut from previous jobs to be involved in this new and exciting venture. Most were working long hours and making big sacrifices. And everyone knew Billy was the son of our major funder.

I was the national sales and marketing manager and needed an assistant, so this young man was assigned to me. In Billy's defence, working as a marketing assistant to a young woman in a department he didn't understand was not great for him either. It was a recipe for disaster.

So ... Billy was habitually late, although I spoke to him many times about it. Each morning, everyone else started at 7:30, and Billy strolled in at 9:15. (Lateness was something your grandfather Roger never tolerated—he had us at church a half-hour early each Sunday because he wanted to make sure we would never be late.)

No amount of reprimanding seemed to fix this problem, so I finally had to give Billy a caution: if he were late again, I would have no choice but to let him go. Imagine how I felt—I was sure William would not be pleased.

Billy made it in on time the following morning, arriving at the office with his dad. When I saw them come in together, I thought I was going to be fired. Sure enough, William came into my office and sat down after asking Billy to join us. I had never been so scared in my life. This was a great job and a fabulous opportunity for me, all blown by this huge mistake.

As it turned out, William had heard about my warning and told Billy that if he couldn't work out how to get in on time, he should be fired.

In front of his dad, I asked Billy what his hopes were for this job. Unsurprisingly, he launched into a passionate speech about how this was not what he wanted and he felt he was wasting his time. I agreed that, although he'd been helpful, his talents were wasted working for me. It turned out he had some ideas for a new division of the company, using his engineering talents. William financed the new endeavour, and it ended up being a revolutionary and very profitable business.

We had a company meeting to let all the staff know about the changes, and everyone was soon on board with the new division. If Billy's tardiness had been allowed to continue much longer, we would have had a team of understandably unhappy employees, given that one person was allowed to set his own schedule while everyone else arranged their lives to be on time.

The new division was so successful Billy and William created an entirely new company later, and Billy asked me to become the vice-president.

As you can imagine, I could have handled the situation differently and alienated Billy completely. But by realizing he was unfulfilled, I was able to help him achieve his goals—and in the end, Billy ended up giving me what I really wanted, which was to become a VP at a very young age.

YOUR ACTION STEP

How long is your fuse? When you're triggered by someone's behaviour, how long do you think about it before you act? For some people, the reaction is almost instantaneous; others will stew for days before deciding what to do.

If you're in the first group, fireproofing your bridges can be as easy (that's a joke; it's never easy) as learning to count to 10, taking three deep breaths, and then saying, "Let's schedule some time to talk about this tomorrow," before leaving the room.

If you are a stewer, your bridges are safer, but there is a price—your focus and sense of well-being are likely to suffer when you're grappling with your next move or trying to manage your frustration. The next time you face this challenge, schedule two 15-minute periods on your calendar to think about and deal with the problem. If you don't come to a solution during those times, schedule a 15-minute chat with a mentor.

BRINGING OUT THE BEST IN CHALLENGING PEOPLE

Mom, I have a person on my team who opposes everything. What do I do?

It's sadly true that some people are difficult to work with, and your success in life will depend in part on managing to work with them anyway.

Consider approaching each potential confrontation with some solid points that show you have thought long and hard, and researched all the options, before settling on what you believe is the correct strategy. If you are working with a team, it is sometimes best to sit with everyone and brainstorm the solution together beforehand. If you take this route, it is also important to review your team's suggestions carefully and let them know why you decided to pursue the action you then set in place. Saying things like "because I think it's best" or "it was my decision to make" may be true, but it can create unnecessary resistance in people who hate being told what to do or who just want to be reassured that their opinions are valued.

Make sure you are not lured into conflicts by someone who just loves to fight. As the adage goes, "Never have a mud fight with a pig, because you'll both get dirty and only the pig will like it."

If you are a high achiever, you will be the target of naysayers who want to bring you down a peg or two. I used to find myself gravitating to these people to try to help them—trust me, don't do it! Gentle suggestions are fine, but don't take them on. "Kill them with kindness" is another great adage, which just means people who love conflict are empowered by it, while they're disarmed by kindness. Rather than engaging, give them space. (If a response is necessary, try something like, "I appreciate you sharing your concerns. I'll give it some thought.") It often catches them off guard, gives them time to think, too, and makes it clear to others that the difficult person is the problem, not you.

You must also be very careful you don't take on their attitudes. Brian Tracy often says, "You are what you think about." If you take on someone else's negativity, it becomes your negativity. As much as possible, spend time with positive people who look for solutions, not problems!

YOUR ACTION STEP

Make a list of the three most positive and the three most negative people in your life.

Can you schedule more time with the most positive and less with the most negative?

If not, can you sandwich the time you must spend with any of the three most negative people in your life between times with the three most positive?

There may be nothing you can do right now to change this ratio. But keeping it in mind as a goal will help you make decisions as you go forward, which may make all the difference over the long term.

part five

YOU AND YOUR CUSTOMERS

Ultimately, your business success comes down to winning the loyalty of the people who buy your products or services.

Getting these relationships right is pivotal to growth—and survival.

RECOVERING FROM A CUSTOMER SERVICE FAILURE

Mom, we really screwed up.
How do I make it up to the customer?

Customer service can make or break a business, especially one that is new or small.

The more everyone on your team remembers how difficult it was to get the customer in the first place, the easier it will be to remember how important it is to keep them. But I know you know this, honey—and we both know things sometimes go wrong anyway.

If you disappoint a customer, first put the problem into perspective. What was the outcome of the error? Was there a financial loss or an impact on the customer's reputation? What did they pay for and expect versus what they received? Were their expectations reasonable?

The answers to these questions should determine how you deal with the problem.

The stakes are high, of course. I worked for a company for many years that went above and beyond service expectations. They implemented a lifetime warranty in an industry where two years was the usual maximum. It was seldom, if ever, that we didn't exceed our customers' expectations—even when we screwed up. Our approach brought us lots of business, and it rarely cost us much, especially when compared to the cost of marketing to bring in new clients. It also made everyone on staff very customer-centric, which gave us a loyal customer base.

Here are some strategies to employ when things go wrong:

1. Identify the real problem. Be sure you are speaking with the correct people to ensure it isn't simply a misunderstanding. In other words, get all the facts.

2. Apologize. But be careful not to go overboard—saying you're sorry 15 times sounds unprofessional.

3. Have a solution in mind when you deliver the apology. If possible, tailor your response to the circumstance and the client's preference. There will be times you need to delay offering a solution until you've had time to think; mentioning that you have to talk to your partner or boss is always a good stalling tactic. But let clients know when you will get back to them.

4. Discuss the solution you have in mind with them to be sure it aligns with their expectations.

5. Deliver the solution quickly—don't make them wait.

The most crucial of all the points above is #4. I recently read a story about a man who bought two Spirit Airlines tickets for a solo cross-country trip. He is very large, and he wanted to have the seat next to him open, so he could sit comfortably without encroaching on a seat mate's space. The airline overbooked the flight (as they all seem to these days) and told him he could not have the second seat as they needed it for another passenger—but "not to worry," as they would refund the cost.

This is a perfect example of missed expectations. He obviously was not concerned about the cost of the second seat; his concern was being comfortable. Of course, the airline now says they will make it right with him, but the damage is done. Bad social media and publicity will cost Spirit untold revenue and make it harder to attract new customers. Don't assume you know what will make your customer happy—discuss the solution and come to an agreement.

Above all else, remember that mistakes happen and all you can do is fix them. If you continue to hear about this instance in your dealings with this customer, read the next chapter on appropriate customer behaviour and firing a customer.

YOUR ACTION STEP

Do you have a "sunshine file"? If not, now is the time to start one. In it, keep every congratulatory or positive thing anyone has ever said or written about you and your work.

When you fail, as you will and must to grow, deal with the problem. Then spend some time with your sunshine file. Don't let one mistake among 1,000 successes ruin your week.

DO YOU NEED A DIVORCE FROM YOUR CUSTOMER?

Mom, I can't seem to make one of my customers happy, and she is taking up so much time!

It usually starts with a problem you created by making a mistake, but sometimes you just can't make a customer happy no matter what you do.

What do you do with this unhappy, unsatisfied customer when she continues to throw an error back at you even after it is addressed?

Sometimes people are most comfortable in the role of victim. We all have some of these people in our lives, and it is often detrimental to our overall well-being. It can even impact our performance—working too hard or stressing too much to try to make a difficult person happy means you have fewer resources to provide service to people who treat you and your team respectfully.

I am reminded of a colleague who told me how he fires clients. What?! Fire clients? Who would do that, you ask?

My friend Andrew was a successful installer of very high-end electronics for the homes of wealthy people. He would sometimes walk away from jobs because of what he called "unhealthy, unprofitable drama."

One time, for example, Andrew presented a proposal to a man who wanted to have his entire house outfitted with 12 TVs, speakers and control systems to work them all. When he looked at Andrew's quote, he mentioned he could get TVs of the same size for quite a bit less at Costco. He wondered aloud what else on the quote was "overpriced." Andrew replied that he would be happy to let the customer pick up and install his own TVs. He also took the quote back and added 10 percent to the bottom line. When the customer saw this, he said, "Hey, what's that for?"

"I can see this project will end up costing me a lot more than I anticipated, and I want to make sure I cover my costs," Andrew replied.

Why did he do that? In his type of business, margins are very tight, and the jobs are often not very lucrative. Knowing which customers will be fair and let you make your margin is an essential skill.

Seth Godin, the author of 18 best-selling books on entrepreneurship, once said, "In general, organizations are afraid to fire customers, no matter how unreasonable. This is a mistake. It is good for you."

Do you know which of your customers are good and which are bad? Can you walk away from the bad ones? Too often, we think we need to take on everyone, so we can get our gross sales up—but if a customer is going to cost you money, you need to walk away. Focus on the customers who are good for your business.

Don't be afraid—cutting a toxic customer loose is good for a company's revenues and the well-being of its people.

YOUR ACTION STEP

I love this one!

Make a list of your top 20 customers by the income they generate.

Now make a list of the 20 customers who take up the most of your time or your team's time.

Are they the same?

If not, make it a weekly action item to think about ways to reallocate focus toward your best customers and away from the time sinks. If appropriate, consider brainstorming this idea with the rest of your team.

part six

MAKING
THE LEAP

You've been dreaming about leaving your
job and starting your own venture.

How do you know when you're ready?
Read on ...

JUST DO IT

■ *Mom, how do I turn my dreams into reality?*

Let me turn this question over to Tony Robbins: "If you talk about it, it's a dream; if you envision it, it's possible; but if you schedule it, it's real."

I am sure you have a friend who has talked for days, weeks—years—about something she is going to do. Eventually. What stops her? Fear? Procrastination? Laziness? It can be a combination of all three, but the saddest part is that it is most often just a lack of effort to make the first move, which is to create a plan.

I can talk candidly about this because I talked for years about writing a book.

What was I missing to complete this dream? Some might say I had no time, as I had a very demanding career and was raising three daughters. But really, I finally realized nothing would happen without a concrete set of action steps to complete.

As Brian Tracy says, "All successful women and men are big dreamers. They imagine what their future could be, ideal in every respect, and then they work every day toward their distant vision, that goal or purpose." They know all they need to do is sit down and map out the steps required to get to the goal.

Think about all the people who defied the odds to do what they do. Do you think J. K. Rowling sat down and said, "I am going to need to be rejected over and over before I become a success?" She had to adapt her strategy each time her manuscript was rejected and think of new ways to get published.

The bottom line? Start! Create small steps. Make commitments to yourself to achieve each level of success. Don't scare yourself into thinking you need to be wildly successful in the first year. Make each step a success and reward yourself for reaching it.

1.   Don't overanalyze—begin. Most people who have an idea for a dream product or service idea spend years just thinking about it. (Until it's time for regret when they see someone else brought it to market.) Think it through, of course, but start taking steps forward, too. Make a list of things you could do to begin. Is it a product? The first step might be to look to see if there are any patents on similar products and what is available in the market today. If it is an idea, google it—just get researching.

2.   Commit time and resources. How much time can you commit to this project? Will it take some financial investment, and, if so, how much? Can you afford it? If not, are there ways you can reduce the launch cost, save up a start-up fund or attract investors?

3.   Set goals with deadlines. For example, if you are writing a book like I did, you'll have to commit to a certain number of words each day.

4. Review your plan with your significant other and make sure they are on board. Let them know how important it is to you and that you will treat it as a second job until it is your full-time job.

5. Save some money so you will have a cushion when it is time to quit your job. This will take some time and significant sacrifice. Yes, you may have to do without Starbucks or a holiday.

When it comes to turning dreams into life,
the three most important things are:

Start!
Reward yourself each step of the way!
Don't give up!

YOUR ACTION STEP

Do step one of the list found earlier in this chapter.

WHEN YOUR INNER ENTREPRENEUR WON'T WAIT

Mom, I just hate my job! What do I do?

"My goal is to build a life I don't need a vacation from."

ROB HILL SR.
Inspirational Speaker

"Your work is going to fill a large part of your life, and the only way to be truly satisfied is to do what you believe is great work. And the only way to do great work is to love what you do. If you haven't found it yet, keep looking. Don't settle."

STEVE JOBS
Co-Founder of Apple

All three of my girls are entrepreneurs, a lot like their mom. (Well, one is a teacher, but I still consider her an entrepreneur, as I will explain later.)

Looking back, all of my career decisions were about building a life around my family. I believe that being an entrepreneur is the best way to build a life you will love. Many, many entrepreneurs are women trying to work around the limitations imposed on them in the corporate world. (Yes, even in this day and age.)

We're usually trying to work out a way to make money and "have it all," which is why I call my daughter the teacher an entrepreneur. Her top priorities are her two small children and her husband. Despite everything on her plate and her commitment to spending time with them, she has found a way to teach, too, because she loves it.

When you are young, with the world in front of you, you may not realize how quickly life happens. Don't be afraid of making changes that move you toward whatever it is that makes you the happiest. Life is short, and regrets are not something you want, especially about letting things come between you and the success you are looking for.

There were many times in my career I truly hated my job. There is short-term hate (today sucked!) and long-term hate (January: I'm dying here! December: Yes, I'm definitely dying here.). When the first situation happened a little too often, I made a plan to adjust my job and my attitude, changing the things I could and accepting the rest, in order to fulfil my goals. In the second, I made a longer-term plan to find work that fulfilled me.

First and foremost, you need to refer to your goals. (Revisit the chapter on goal setting if you don't feel completely clear on this.)

Wherever you are, consider these potential steps toward positive change:

1. Is there a remedy for the unhappiness in your workplace? Are there changes you could make that would improve the situation? What is it, exactly, that is making you miserable? Articulate the problems and then work with anyone with influence to find out if changes can be made.

2. Look around at your options. What could you do that would be better for you? Look at other jobs being offered. Perhaps it is time to start the side project that will truly make your dreams come true. There are periods in life when our money and our fulfilment come from different sources, and that's okay—sometimes we need more fulfilment rather than a new, shinier way to earn money. And in time, you can build your "side hustle" into your primary source of income, and then—if it's what you want—even more.

3. If you realize that fixing your current job is unlikely, thoughtfully share your issues with your boss. Let someone know that you are so unhappy you are considering leaving. I've had a few instances when I was shocked and upset when someone quit without letting me know they were unhappy, as I believe we could have fixed the problem. Don't underestimate how much the people above you can miss; they may be so overwhelmed themselves that they don't see the problems you're experiencing. Be careful here, of course—this tactic can backfire, so you'll want to be prepared to lose your job (step #2).

It is so important to be happy with your work, not just for your well-being but because your team's productivity is impacted by how happy you are. If you are disillusioned or don't feel valued, you'll drag yourself around all day, and it will affect everything in your life. I know some people are afraid of change. However, I can't emphasize enough how important it is to love what you do and feel like you are contributing.

In her poem "The Dash," Linda Ellis imagines looking at a gravestone with the awareness that it is the dash between the year we are born and the year we die that signifies everything worth knowing about our lives. There is nothing more important than looking after your dash!

These stats will make you think about how you spend your work life:

1.   25% of employees say work is their main source of stress.

2.   40% say their job is "very or extremely stressful."

3.   The average North American spends **90,000 HOURS** at work over a 50-year career.

Source: *Business Insider*

Often the toughest part is the decision to start making a change. Once you do, you'll need to set some time aside each week. What will you need to do to get you started? Consider dedicating five hours a week (just one hour each day) to creating an action list to achieve a better job or to make the changes that will allow you to enjoy your current job.

1.   Dream big. What is it that you always wanted to do? I decided I wanted to be a ski instructor when I grew up, so when I was 50, I took lessons and the test required to do so. It helped me to understand that nothing is entirely out of reach. What would you do if you could not fail? What would you do if you had all the time and money in the world?

2.   Make a list of the action steps you will need to take to get there.

3.   Look at the list and your calendar and set deadlines for each of those action steps.

4.   Tell someone what you are doing. Accountability is extremely motivating.

Whatever you do, don't quit! If you realize that you may have gone in the wrong direction, don't quit the journey. Create a new list of goals and deadlines and get to it.

Steve Jobs also said, "I'm convinced that about half of what separates the successful entrepreneur from the non-successful ones is pure perseverance."

Life is about choices—choose happiness and fulfilment!

YOUR ACTION STEP

Break out your notebook and spend 10 minutes making a list of anything that might be stopping you from making positive changes in your life right now. It could be financial fears, ego fears, fear of displeasing your family, fear of not being the kind of person who can make challenging situations work—there are an endless number of possibilities for this one.

To help identify your top fears, think about your "worst-case scenarios." What's the very worst thing you can imagine happening? The next worst thing? Keep going until you run out of steam or 10 minutes is up.

For extra credit, google "Linda Ellis The Dash," read her inspiring poem, and think about anything you'd like to change while you still can.

THE IMPORTANCE OF A PLAN

Mom, why do I get so pumped up when I am with certain people and then lose all my faith when I'm with others?

According to *Entrepreneur*[1] magazine, an entrepreneur is "a person who starts a business and is willing to risk loss in order to make money," or "one who organizes, manages, and assumes the risk of a business." The key word in both definitions is RISK. This means that the upsides you experience will always come with downsides or possibly even failures. The bottom line is that you are in uncharted waters and are likely to experience setbacks and reversals. Entrepreneurship has also been described as "a business rollercoaster." With it comes feelings of, "What am I doing?!"

I was recently at a networking event where the speaker talked about the journeys of young, entrepreneurial women and how their paths are not always smooth. When she asked for questions, someone asked for advice on staying positive during negative times. Like you, the woman who asked for advice mentioned that when she was with certain people, she felt she was totally on the right path. But when confronted by her father, who drilled her with questions about how she was going to pay the bills with this "so-called" new job, she felt like she might, in fact, be on the wrong track.

The speaker replied that these feelings are common and that the ability to stay positive and confident is a reflection of how prepared you are to answer tough questions.

Do you stumble and say something like "We will see" when you're faced with challenging questions of this nature? If so, does this prompt more questions? Or do you explain that it is all in the business plan you have prepared? When you have a plan and can answer questions intelligently and in detail, you will also experience greater confidence in everything you do. If you could say with certainty that you will be in the black in the next 18 months and your research shows you will easily be able to double your sales in three years, enabling you to add one more full-time person to the team, it's likely you'll shut the naysayer down fast.

Having a business plan, even if it is the most basic of plans, is essential to help you confidently pitch your case.

But let's face it—young entrepreneurs often rely on the "I have more money coming in than going out" type of plan. Sound familiar? If so, you are bound to cave under pressure. Many entrepreneurs say they don't have time to make a business plan. Trust me on this one—it is critical to your future to take the time. How will you grow without it? How do you know how you will pay the bills without it? If you don't know these essentials, you'll spend too much energy managing your anxiety rather than investing your energy in growing your business.

Naysayers are among the best motivations we can have. How many of us would move mountains to prove that we can do this and make it profitable? Harness their negativity and make it work positively for you.

Zig Ziglar once said, "Sometimes adversity is what you need to face in order to be successful."

So how do you create a business plan? There are many books out there on this subject, but start small. Don't get too carried away with details. The most important part of a good business plan is the financials. Talk to your accountant. I hope you have one—they are not expensive and can save you lots of money. If you don't, please put this book down and find one now. Have her provide you with a spreadsheet showing current revenue and expenses. Take this information and forecast sales and expenses out two, three and five years. This is one of the most important exercises you can do and will tell you a great deal about yourself and your business.

The next step is to analyze the spreadsheet. Does it make sense? In other words, can you achieve your sales goals with the people you have, or do you need more? If so, have you included this cost? This is a blueprint for your business, so make sure the information is solid.

Finally, be grateful for the naysayers in your life, but surround yourself with cheerleaders because they can be your best source of strength in tough times. Being an entrepreneur means facing challenges, and when you do, you will need the encouragement of people who believe in you. You might meet a stranger at a networking event who goes on to become your biggest support. Be honest with people. You will be astonished how easy this is to explain in a group of entrepreneurs.

YOUR ACTION STEP

Find your cheerleaders and ask for help! Think about who you could call today, and if no one comes to mind, find a networking group and join as soon as you can. Facebook groups can be great for inspiration, but there is nothing that replaces face-to-face social time.

POLISHING YOUR PITCH

> *Mom, I need a better response when people ask me about my business. I don't want to be like the guy I met on the weekend who rambled on and on until I had to excuse myself to end his misery. Help!?*

You need an elevator pitch, designed to provide the most important facts in the average time you'd spend with someone in an elevator. (That's between 30 and 60 seconds, in case you're wondering.) This is your pitch about you and your product or service, and it is designed to give listeners just enough essential information to make them want more.

The key elements in a powerful elevator pitch are passion and preparedness, the two factors that will convince your listeners you will achieve your goals. Some elevator pitches are easy, like mine right now: "I am a writer and will publish a book this year about the skills I learned building two successful businesses."

Some pitches are more complex, but the key is to briefly outline the steps you took to put your passion into a plan.

Here are the key elements in an effective pitch:

1. Does your business solve a problem? If so, state it. It may be simple, like, "There are no good Indian restaurants in my city." Whatever it is, make sure it is stated clearly and succinctly. There is nothing worse than losing someone in the first sentence. Instead of starting with something like "I analyze the clinical aspects of microorganisms, including the host response to these agents …," you could say, "I am one of the only people in the region analyzing bacteria and their impact on the new superbugs." In other words, start with a problem most people will relate to, like a superbug rather than a "host response."

2. The second sentence should be about how you will solve the problem. "There are no good Indian restaurants here, so I am opening one." Many people start with the solution (opening an Indian restaurant), and it could be that the person listening does not know of the problem (in theory, there could be a half-dozen good Indian restaurants nearby), so this is imperative.

3. Mention your target customer and their proximity. Using the same example, perhaps you are opening a southern-style Indian food restaurant and have found that immigration of people from this region is the highest in the neighbourhood you've chosen. In the earlier example, our researcher might add that her work is intended to better equip hospitals to stop infection outbreaks in local regions.

4. Next, describe who you will be competing against and how you will make yourself different and better. Who is on your team? Do you have an Indian chef who has recently come from a well-known restaurant? Is this person from South India?

That's your elevator pitch, but there is one more element you need to have prepared in case you run into your ideal investor or potential partner or just your worried parent. You must be able to quickly explain how you've analyzed the start-up and running costs in your business plans, to identify that you will be able to make back your investment in *X* number of months or years. (See the previous chapter on creating a business plan if you happened to get here first.) Work through the steps with your plan in hand. Remember—no more than a minute. Your passion should show through, and it should feel natural, so practice it a few times. Then go get 'em!

YOUR ACTION STEP

Get out your calendar and schedule 10 minutes for each of the questions in this chapter over the next five business days. There is nothing more important you can do for your business, so it should be easy to make this task a priority.

If you run into trouble, ask to exchange some skill time with a friend or colleague who has strong marketing chops and run through your challenges together.

THE ENTREPRENEUR'S SUPERPOWER— BECOMING COMFORTABLE WITH DISCOMFORT

> Mom, a friend who owns a small business recently asked me how I manage when I must do something that makes me extremely uncomfortable, such as taking a big financial risk. She's great at planning and execution, but not so great at taking risks. I'd love to pass on your advice, too, because I know you were in similar situations many times while growing your companies.

The true test of an entrepreneur is the ability to feel comfortable being uncomfortable. What does that mean exactly?

First of all, when you feel uncomfortable, remember that it is normal—but meaningless. In other words, it is not the universe trying to let you know you're about to do something stupid. It's plain old nerves. We often need to make ourselves uncomfortable to get to that next level.

Let's say you are a creative type. You love being behind the camera but being in front of it scares the crap out of you—now you have to do it to promote your business. Only a tiny percentage of people love being in the limelight. Even those who seem to have it all together when addressing a crowd are often people who started out scared to death to speak in public or even to do live chats on Facebook. No matter how polished they look today, they're people just like you.

What about asking for the sale? Does this make you uncomfortable? Growing your business is often scary. What if you mess it up? What if you have miscalculated and the strategy you thought would work flops?

Sometimes the discomfort comes from something as simple as telling your family your business idea. You've prepared and have the facts ready for the naysayer who has been unhappy in his job for 30 years but wouldn't dream about leaving it, who says things like, "How can you think that will make money?" or, "How can you even think about leaving your (well-paying) job?!" If you can get comfortable being uncomfortable, you can deliver the answers you've prepared to these questions confidently. You won't let anyone intimidate you into thinking your ideas are not good, and you'll make sure they understand that you've done your homework. You'll show them this is not a lark for you, but a mission for which you are ready.

So how do you get comfortable with discomfort? By being prepared and by doing it over and over again, getting better and better at it each time, until it just doesn't freak you out anymore.

Take a few minutes to make a list of the times you went out on a limb to try something new and it was a home run for you or your business. How did you feel going into those changes? Do you remember being scared? How did you feel afterwards? Like Superwoman, right? Often, when we look back on things that stretched us, we realize it wasn't really all that bad. Why would this time be different? It's not. Regularly revisit memories of the times you powered through, and it will make your current discomfort easier to face.

Is there something today that you know you need to do but are nervous about trying? Consider asking someone to help you through it—to go with you, stand by you and just encourage you along the way.

None of this is easy, mind you. Being an entrepreneur is tough stuff and often more difficult than anything else in life you'll face. You may need to dig deep and go back to your "why"—if you're an entrepreneur because it helps you to spend more time with your family, for instance, draw on that thought when you are wading through the hard parts.

YOUR ACTION STEP

Think of something that makes you feel awkward or nervous, and then do it. Is it offering an acquaintance a compliment or thanking them for a recent action that made your day better? Is it introducing yourself to a neighbour you don't know? Saying hi to a random stranger? Trying a new dance?

Every time you do something hard, you expand your abilities. Start right now, and don't ever stop.

PROTECTING YOUR REVENUES FROM INNOCENT PREDATORS

Mom, how do I let my friends know that I can't afford to give out free advice?

Giving away your services is not good for your business, and it devalues your worth, to others and yourself. But I'm sure everyone with any measure of skill or success has run into this problem.

Imagine someone who starts a digital marketing company and spends five years learning everything she needs to know to provide services and advice to organizations that want a branding presence. To most of her friends and family, she is now the one who is "good at websites." Lots of people need this service, but not many want to pay for it, especially those who don't understand the necessity of marketing. So, she gets cornered at parties and family gatherings by plumbers, lawyers and accountants who are having trouble acquiring clients. You know the ones.

"HOW DO YOU SECURE A DOMAIN NAME?"
"HOW DO I MAKE A LOGO?"

Before she knows it, the party and her hard-earned time off have turned into a work event, and she's spent the last hour telling a highly paid professional what he needs to know. For free.

My solution? Turn this request around. If someone asks for help, tell them you would be happy to meet with them in your office or theirs. Offer to send along your rate sheet, and if they offer a service you need, you can even mention you'd be happy to do a contra deal. If you have a toilet that's running, and your plumber neighbour needs advice on pulling together a basic website, you might be able to arrange a trade. Win-win.

If you don't have a rate sheet, you need one—now, today! It is impossible to let people know with confidence how much your services are worth without having it in black and white. Establishing your value is one of the most important things you can do. If you don't know where to start, can you get a rate sheet from others in your line of work? What about others in similar industries?

The point is: if you have a sought-after skill set you've spent time developing so that you can pay your mortgage with it, don't give it away.

YOUR ACTION STEP

When was the last time someone talked you into giving free advice? Are you a bit annoyed that you got sucked into it? Unless it is your grandma, you should be. Today, email an invoice to the person involved. On it, note the time you spent and your hourly rate, with the amount zeroed out by subtracting a negative amount for something like an "initial complimentary consultation for friend or family member."

Let the person know that you have an excellent accounting system that tracks all your hours by assigning a rate for that hour.

This way, they'll understand the value of your gifted services and get the gentle but essential message that future services will be followed by an invoice on which the bottom line isn't zero.

EXPANSION WHEN?

Mom, I am run off my feet.
Should I hire someone?

With a one-person operation, it can be incredibly stressful to think about the cost of hiring your first employee. It can also be time-consuming to train someone and feel like it is more work than it is worth, at least initially. However, it is sometimes crucial to get an extra pair of hands onboard to help you get to that next level.

First, you need to have your vision clearly set out. Pro tip: make sure it is *your* vision and not someone else's idea of success. Maybe you are happy right where you are, and your revenues and income are enough to pay your bills—you just need to learn to say no to new opportunities and clients when your calendar is full. (If so, you can just skip this chapter for now, and move on to the next.) However, if your goals include creating a company that not only pays your way but rewards others you have hand-selected to share your journey, I have a few things for you to think about.

Figure out what it is you want this new person to do. Take a couple of weeks and journal every day. What are you doing with each hour? How do you feel when you are doing it? When you feel like you have a handle on your pain points and know exactly how you're spending your own time, move on to the following steps:

1.   Whatever you do, don't hand off the duties unique to you. If you are a motivational speaker, for instance, don't hire another motivational speaker. You'd be surprised how often people think the solution to their capacity problem is another person just like them, when they really need someone who has a whole different set of skills and perspectives. You're not hiring a new friend.

2.   Do you know what you are good at and what you are not good at? Be honest with yourself. Pro tip #2: the things we procrastinate on are often the things we are not good at. Again, write it all down.

3.   What are the things you could be doing to generate more revenue if you handed off some of your current work to someone else? For example, if you added a blog to your website, could it create more business? Add that to the list.

At the end of one week, take a look at your notes and create a "perfect employee" job description. You should now be able to calculate how much time you need someone. It may be part-time or even casual (by the hour or on contract) in the beginning. This is also sometimes the best way to find out if the person you hire will fit in with your company. Consider hiring for 10 to 20 hours a week at first to cover some of the duties you don't want to do, then ease into more if it is working out.

Don't hire someone who has never worked for a small business, particularly if they've only had large corporation, Fortune 500-type experience. In a start-up, early hires usually get the coffee and empty the garbage—you don't want to end up doing it because the person you've employed feels it's beneath them.

Above all else, make sure the person you decide to hire understands and is aligned with your culture and values. If your company sells to stay-at-home moms, someone from Wall Street is probably not a good fit.

Often, the best early hires are accountants, web design and social media experts, or someone who is just very organized and focused on the details. These are typically not skills that are common among entrepreneurial women and are aspects of running a business that can be incredibly time-consuming, especially for amateurs.

Finally, try to collaborate or outsource as much as you can. If you are a fashion designer and need a photographer for a one-time shoot, see if you can swap some time to create a win-win.

Remember, hiring is a hit-and-miss exercise. Someone can look fabulous on a resume and even interview as the absolute best choice—but you won't know if they're a good fit until you work with them. On your side of the street, be sure you give detailed, clear instructions about what you expect and give regular feedback. (By regular, I don't mean once a quarter but every day, especially at first.) What are the job's key performance indicators, the tasks and outcomes that will be the measures of the employee's success? How will you measure these indicators?

And don't forget that whoever you hire will not be you. Give him or her a bit of slack in the beginning and above all, be honest at all times.

YOUR ACTION STEP

Spend 10 minutes making a list of the things you do that you're not particularly good at or don't enjoy. Can you hire a virtual assistant, an accountant or a subcontractor (such as a freelance writer, editor or marketing consultant) to outsource these responsibilities to?

In other words, are there responsibilities you can outsource before you hire someone on a committed full- or part-time basis?

FACING NEW CHALLENGES

Mom, how do I get my confidence up when approaching a new business situation?

I recently had the opportunity to be a marshal for the BC Downhill mountain bike race. I was positioned at a difficult bend that included a jump. It was one of the two trickiest sections of the course, with a six-foot drop that couldn't be seen from the entrance, in an area so steep I had trouble walking and had to hang onto trees to accomplish the trek.

It was fascinating to see how each of the more than 100 riders approached this section. Some were new to the sport while others, the elites, were easy to identify—they went over the blind jump with no hesitation. They had obviously done this so many times and knew they had the skill to conquer whatever landing presented itself. Other riders took an easier side entrance, slowing their time. They had not had the experience on their bike necessary to feel confident about mastering the challenge.

What is the difference between these two types of riders? I think most coaches would say it is a mix of skill and time on the bike.

Just like in business. If you are a skilful business person, you didn't just wake up that way one day. You spent time in the trenches, learned from mistakes, fell down and got back up. Through perseverance, you became what you are today.

The important thing to remember as you face any new challenge is that those you revere in your field didn't start their journey yesterday. At one time, they were just like you, new to the industry, field or process that you are now trying to master.

YOUR ACTION STEP

What is your learning edge today?

What do you need to move from beginner to elite in this situation? Is it "time on the bike"? Is it research? More education?

Take 10 minutes to think about what you need in order to feel confident. Make time on your calendar and then go and get it.

FILLING YOUR SKILLS GAPS

Mom, I'm feeling stretched too thin, and I'm afraid my business is suffering because of it. How do I stop myself from wearing too many hats?

When you start your own business, it's usually because you have a passion for something. Someone starts a digital marketing company because she built websites for all her friends and family and decided she loves it. But being good at making websites does not make her good at sales, accounting or negotiating lease rates ... I think you get the picture.

I was good at sales. I was a talker, and a persuader, and I developed a great business. I was well respected for my sales abilities. What I was terrible at was managing my finances. When the business took off, I was even worse at it. Money was coming in; less money was going out—what was the problem?

When your dad realized we had a thriving business, he started to pay closer attention to the money, and I learned it was quite a mess. He ended up taking over the finances and hired a skilled accountant—after that, things were great.

Here's my point: the sooner you recognize your strengths and weaknesses and hire great people who make up for your weaknesses, the better off you will be.

As Microsoft founder Bill Gates said to a graduating class, "I had to learn to recognize and appreciate people's different talents. The sooner you can do this, if you don't already, the richer your life will be." He went on to say that people are much more productive if they surround themselves with others who can teach, challenge and push them to be better.

When you decide to add to your team, make sure you are adding people who complement what you already offer.

This is teamwork.

YOUR ACTION STEP

Take 10 minutes to make a list of the skills and talents you bring to your professional life.

Grab a highlighter or pencil crayon and go through your calendar for the last week, highlighting all the activities that drew on these skills and talents.

Of the activities that are not highlighted, ask yourself which could be better done by someone else with different skills.

part seven

BUILDING AN A-TEAM

When your business grows beyond your capacities, you've reached the point at which only effective leadership, hiring, training, mentoring and inspirational skills can take you to the next level.

WHEN THE WORLD LAUGHS WITH YOU

Mom, how do I lighten things up and get some fun happening at the office for my team?

"You may be feeling lazy today, but remember, you have a long way to go to catch up with the person who named the fireplace."

JASON MILLER
@longwall26

Yes, I stuck a joke in there to make you laugh and make my point—don't underestimate how important humour is in the workplace!

Research has shown that laughter has healing properties. It is a natural stress reliever and has even been linked to pain relief. Have you ever felt almost euphoric after a really good laugh? It's like you've pushed all the stale air out of the room and replaced it with great, clean, positive oxygen.

I think of laughter as internal jogging; it provides more stamina. It can also be a great stimulant to get the creative juices flowing for groups. I have known many successful organizations that encourage silliness, play and laughter to help build strong teams.

If you are a team leader, why not share the silly things you do, like forgetting your keys in a strange place or leaving your phone in a bathroom? We all do things like this; laughing at our foibles lightens the atmosphere and makes it easier for people to be themselves. I once had my phone in my back pocket in the washroom, and guess what? It fell out and landed in the toilet. I was so stressed thinking about what I was going to tell my team because we were at a trade show and needed that phone. But I finally emerged from the bathroom and let them know what I had done. We all had a great laugh about it, which eased my stress and brightened their days, too.

Secondly, ask yourself what you're bringing to your workplace. We all know people who constantly have a scowl on their faces. They seem to have continuous troubles they love to tell you about. (I don't mean people who are in the midst of a real crisis or who have mental health issues. That's another chapter. I mean people who just see the glass as half-empty, all the time.) To avoid ever becoming this type of person, please listen to yourself when you speak. Some days, it's easy to start going on about all the terrible things that have happened to you. Stop. Your mind is a wonderful thing but fill it with negative thoughts and it's too easy to become a negative person. As former Vancouver police chief Jamie Graham once said, "No one wants to follow a pessimist."

Everyone has troubles—life is full of them. Next time you are having one of those days, change your attitude by doing something good for yourself. Don't dwell on the troubles; shake it off and start again. Above all, don't complain or tell anyone in your office. (If you feel the need to vent, call your mom— then you have 10 minutes to process, and you're paying for the coffee.)

Look for the good in your day and make it your focus. A gratitude journal is a great way to develop the habit of acknowledging and celebrating the positive in your life. Having accountability partners is also a good idea— if you start heading down the negative road, they can bring you back, and vice versa.

Life is short. Enjoy it at all times. Remember, it is a choice!

YOUR ACTION STEP

Get a gratitude journal. You probably have a lovely notebook lying around waiting to be used, but if not, put one on your shopping list. (It doesn't have to cost $20, but if $20 won't hurt your budget, it's nice to have something you're grateful to write in.)

Decide when you will write in it each day, and how many entries you'll make.

Do it. Promise yourself you'll never miss two days in a row. If you miss a week because both kids have the flu or you're on vacation, start again as soon as you remember.

The more you do it, the better your day and your life will be. It's scientifically proven.

STAYING POSITIVE, CONNECTED AND CURRENT

> *Mom, how do I stay positive and up to date on advances in our field while I'm working so hard? How do I encourage the people on my team to do the same?*

Read, read, read—and then read some more.

I am an avid reader of business books. While travelling more than 100,000 kilometres each year for more than 10 years, I spent thousands of hours in airports browsing in bookstores. I have many, many business books and, to this day, I always pick up the latest and greatest. (You'll find a list of some of my favourites at the back of this book.)

I had an inspirational boss for two decades who had his upper management team do reports on books he suggested. I have to say that, while I learned so much while studying for my master's degree in sales and marketing, I learned as much or more from the time I've spent reading. And never underestimate what you can learn from a successful person in a completely different industry.

Someone on your team may tell you they "don't read." It's not a good excuse these days, as there are some amazing audiobooks and podcasts available. No money for books? Check out the local library—they are full of free reading material, and you can download e-books and audio books at home. Sign up for the free *Entrepreneur* magazine newsletter, which often provides great articles and book recommendations.

Anyone who can pull out an example of something Warren Buffett did, or quotes from other successful leaders who have gone before, will be respected for it by their boss, customers and peers.

As a founder, it's also essential that you join local networking groups to meet other entrepreneurs. This is hugely positive as you may find like-minded people who you can collaborate with to grow your business and who will help you stay current and motivated. As well, attend any sales training offered in your city or online. You will always get something out of it and, even if it is a small nugget, it could translate into $$$ down the road.

As an entrepreneur, personal development is critical to your success, providing insights that keep you motivated as well as skills and knowledge that can keep you ahead of your competition.

YOUR ACTION STEP

You decide. What are you going to do in the next month to make yourself better at your profession?

Order a book, schedule 20 minutes to watch a TED talk, attend a training session.

For now, your action step is just to decide what it is going to be and to schedule it on your calendar.

part eight

SALES SUPERPOWERS FOR YOU AND YOUR TEAM

Call it sales, marketing, promotion or simply success—we ultimately win or lose by convincing others they need what we offer.

SALES GOALS AND YOUR WHY

Mom, how can I keep my sales motivation up? Some days I feel like I am on fire — other days, it all comes to a screeching halt!!

My motivation always comes back to my "why."

The why is something that everyone in sales and marketing—and every other challenging career—needs to determine. For me, it was always my family. From a very early stage in my career, I tried to work out how I could be home more with my kids.

Especially if you don't love the product or service you're selling, you need to regularly remind yourself of your own why to reconnect with your passion, enthusiasm and determination. Maybe you need to have photos or other images in front of you. Before you get back on the phone or in front of a prospect, create a paradigm shift and make sure you are projecting your passion by focusing on your why.

At the same time, if you work for someone else, don't lose sight of your goals set by those above you.

- Do you know what your boss is responsible for in achieving sales goals? What is his or her role in your success?

- Did your boss set the goals or were they set by those above?

- Are the goals realistic?

Have you analyzed how you're doing? Don't bury your head in the sand and just go out and try to sell. Know what you need to sell each month and then break it down even further: how much do you need to sell every week? Every day?

When I was in sales, as you know, I mostly sold high-end, in-ceiling speakers. To stay motivated, I needed to break my targets down by how many speakers I needed to sell each day. Once I did, the challenge became real.

You also need to measure your performance. If you need to sell 100 speakers each day and you are consistently selling 50, you need to have a meeting with your boss. Is the expectation unrealistic, or are you doing something wrong? It is better to meet this head on than to get fired over it. Request help and ask which members of the team are meeting their quotas so you can learn from them.

Be proactive. Do not assume things will get better on their own—ask for help early and you will be respected for it. Remember that sales is almost always a team sport, and team members must work together to achieve their goals.

YOUR ACTION STEP

What's your why? Spend 10 minutes writing about why your why is your why.

For extra credit, identify one thing you could do right now to help keep your why front of mind whenever you reach for the phone or meet with a new client.

HIRING AND INSPIRING YOUR SALES TEAM

> Mom, I don't feel I know much about sales. How do I hire the right people and inspire my sales team to get our products out there?

I have been managing sales people for over 20 years, and when I meet people who are truly 100 percent behind their product or service, I always hope their employer is paying them big money—because that is definitely what they're worth.

What is it that makes these people so happy and passionate about what they're selling? Why do they look like they can't wait to get to work? There are two primary factors—personal drive and passion for their product or service.

As sales managers, how do we identify that drive and impart that passion? Do our people believe in our product or service as much as we do? Is it just a job for them, or do they really care about what they are selling? It may sound simplistic, but sales are not easy—if we don't have strong feelings for the product or service we are selling, we won't be successful.

When you look at the members of your sales team, these are important questions to ask. How did they end up on your team? Are they still happy with what they are doing, or have they developed "sales fatigue"? As I travelled all over the world making sales calls with territory reps, I often wondered how they got to where they were. As a curious person, I usually asked. As we all know, there are lots of great salespeople—but there are others I will call "lost in the profession." They were attracted to the job because someone told them it would be easy, or the hours were flexible. Without passion, they've floundered.

Are your people clear on the sales presentation process? Can they replicate it naturally and enthusiastically, time after time after time? Sales is a game, and often a difficult one.

How many "nos" does it take to get to a "yes"? Do your salespeople sometimes race through their presentations, trying to get to yes faster by rushing through the inevitable nos? Who wants to admit to making 10 sales calls and being turned down flat by every prospect? But Michael Jordan offers this unparalleled lesson in how to talk about our failures and the importance of showing up for the nos:

"I've missed more than 9,000 shots in my career. I've lost almost 300 games. Twenty-six times, I've been trusted to take the game-winning shot and missed. I've failed over and over again in my life. And that is why I succeed."

When hiring, remember it is next to impossible to turn a pessimist into an optimist and that salespeople must be optimists. As billionaire inventor and investor Elon Musk said, "If you wake up in the morning and think the future is going to be better, it is a bright day. Otherwise, it's not."

I recently came across a story about a 92-year-old, partially blind woman who was being shown the room she would occupy for the rest of her years. As she turned a corner, she said, "I love it." The nurse said, "Sorry, but you are not in it yet. How can you say you love it?" With a smile, the elderly lady said, "It's easy. I have already decided I will love it and so I love it."

We can choose how we will feel about something long before we experience it. If we choose to love something we will love it—so, as employers, it's important to choose team members who know how to love their work.

YOUR ACTION STEP

This is a tough one: think about what you're modelling for the people around you. Be honest with yourself. Are you doing everything you can to model optimism to your team?

Spend 10 minutes journaling in your notebook about how you might inspire more optimism in the people who look to you to set the tone for your business.

WHAT IT MEANS TO BE GREAT IN SALES TODAY

> *Mom, I don't feel particularly good at sales, and as you've said many times, being able to sell yourself and your business is critical to the success of any entrepreneur. How will I make it?*

We all know some exceptionally talented salespeople—my dad referred to them as the ones with "the gift of gab." They know just what to say to get people to do whatever it is they want them to do. Does that mean that, if we don't have that particular gift, we can't be effective at marketing our business?

I don't think so. I don't believe I was a particularly great salesperson, even though I spent my entire career in sales, managed international sales teams and was considered one of the best in the world in my field.

How did I do it? I think those of us with less of the "gift of gab" need to be able to do the following:

1. You must believe in what you are selling. If you don't, people will not buy it. Are you selling something that you would buy yourself if money were no object? If not, you may have trouble convincing someone else to do so.

2. Be authentic. I truly believe that no one is tricked into buying something. You must be truthful and express yourself genuinely at all times. Be the real you. If you are not "salesy," don't try to be. Own who you are and don't apologize. Make sure you add something of yourself to the process: where you came from, why you are doing this. Try to find some common ground and build on it. It goes a long way toward developing a relationship. People buy from other people.

3. Work hard. Hard work beats talent every time. If you are not gifted with the sales gene, you need to perfect your pitch and make sure you understand everything about what you are selling. Learn from the best—have you read all the sales books out there? If not, check out my recommendations at the end of this book. Buy them, read them and read them again!

4. Don't rattle off your pitch without listening to the customer. Talk with them, not at them.

5. Find out what your customers' pain points are. That is, what are their problems or irritations, and how does the product or service you're providing solve or ease them? If they are considering a switch from another brand or product, make sure you know everything about it. But never, never, never say negative things about your competitors or their products—it serves no purpose

and makes you look bad. Instead, emphasize the benefits of your offerings and the reasons people like them.

6. Be prepared and organized. If you need to pull up some information, have it readily at hand to look professional. Make sure you present yourself as if this is the most important thing you could be doing.

7. Don't sell with your wallet. In other words, if you could only imagine spending $2,000 on something, you may not realize that your customer was looking for $10,000 quality.

8. If you are not successful with a prospect, make sure you ask why. Again, be authentic. Make it simple and easy to let you know what caused them to say no.

9. Don't let yourself feel guilty or defeated. Accept that you will fail; people will say no, and it is not personal. Pick yourself up and move on to the next prospect.

10. Don't give up too soon. What many people don't realize is that the sales process often takes time. Not everyone will want what you are selling today. It may have nothing to do with your product, price or personality. It may have to do with them not being ready yet. Ask if you may follow up and if so, make sure you do!

I think the days of the hard-sell salesperson are behind us. Most people can obtain any and all information on the internet, so old-school sales tricks are no longer effective. Informed buyers are looking for educated salespeople who offer solutions and put customer service first in the process.

This is great news for those of us without the hard-sell skills. If we understand our product, work hard, are honest about what we offer and provide great support after the sale, we'll be great salespeople.

YOUR ACTION STEP

Read through the steps in this chapter and decide which one is closest to your most significant personal challenge right now. Decide on a strategy to help you develop in this area, and schedule time on your calendar in the coming months to make it happen.

part nine

WHEN TIMES GET TOUGH

Anyone can make it through the easy times. The people we think of as successful have made it through the tough times, too, over and over again.

Here's what you need to do when those challenges arrive.

MANAGING MISTAKES WITH GRACE

Mom, how do I deal with my errors in business?

Own up. You'll be an inspiration to everyone who knows you because if you aren't making mistakes, you are not trying hard enough. As an avid snow skier, I know that if I don't fall from time to time it's because I'm slacking off. In business, it's easy to get in the habit of treading lightly and trying not to make any mistakes, but guess what? It doesn't move you forward.

Richard Branson's famous adage, "Screw it; let's do it!" is a prime example of this philosophy. As he says, "While this attitude has helped us build hundreds of companies, it hasn't always resulted in success." Many famously successful business people have gone bankrupt several times in their careers. Mistakes and other failures can be stepping stones on the way to greatness.

Richard Branson also said, "You don't learn to walk by following the rules, you learn by doing and by falling over."

Now, this can be a difficult one if you're employed by someone else. If you are taking risks, you need to make sure your boss is on your side. If you are your own boss, however, this is something you should do regularly—use your gut feelings to know when to go for it.

When mistakes do happen, always be honest and admit to them. This can take some courage at first, I know—most people are afraid to 'fess up to something that goes wrong until they've practised doing so a few times. It's an essential skill to develop.

As someone who has managed people for a long time, I can assure you it is much better and more comforting to hear from employees that they've messed up than it is to find out later. Present the problem, the solution and the lesson that was learned, at the earliest, to your supervisor.

Steve Jobs said it well: "Sometimes when you innovate, you make mistakes. It is best to admit them quickly and get on with improving your other innovations."

The key here is to quickly identify the mistake, not cover it up. I have made a lot of mistakes in my career, some of which woke me up in the middle of the night and made me blurt, "Oh, crap!" aloud. But the important thing is that I learned from them and can say I will never make them again.

If you have made a leadership mistake in your business, get your employees in immediately to admit to it and work on a plan to fix it or make a change in direction.

If your team or company makes a mistake with a customer or another stakeholder (like your bank or a supplier), whatever you do, DO NOT blame any person specifically. Even if you know it is one person's responsibility, make it a team effort and always refrain from throwing others under the bus. See the chapter on customer service recovery, take charge and offer solutions instead of hashing out what has already been identified as the problem.

YOUR ACTION STEP

What was your last truly epic error? Spend 10 minutes writing about what you learned.

Is there anything else that could have taught you these lessons quite so effectively?

SILENCING NEGATIVE MENTAL CHATTER

Mom, how do I deal with negative feelings, especially after a setback?

Throughout your life, your attitude will determine whether or not you succeed in achieving your goals.

Researchers say we have between 50,000 and 70,000 thoughts per day. That means we have up to 70,000 chances to build ourselves up or talk ourselves out of success. Mind your mind!

Your thoughts will dictate how you feel. Do you ever realize you are dwelling on something in a way that it is making you depressed? Of course, you do! You would not be an entrepreneur if you didn't.

You may worry about how a client feels about you, based on a conversation that you misinterpreted on Friday afternoon. On Monday, you'll figure out your error, but in the meantime, it ruins your weekend. Instead of letting a misunderstanding get in the way of your happiness, put it out of your mind and focus on the positive. If you can't, call and clarify your understanding of the situation.

Sports therapists will tell you that you always need to visualize yourself achieving your goal. As an aggressive skier, I always like to ski with the best on the mountain, challenging myself to ski the hardest runs. I can always tell how I will ski a run by how I have talked to myself at the top. The times I've barely made it down are the times I forgot to psych myself up, imagining that I will ski like one of the best skiers I have ever seen.

This kind of visualization is scientifically proven to work. Your self-talk about your business needs to be the same. Picture the outcome you want and how you will achieve it, and then go into it with complete confidence that you will achieve the end goal.

If you're trying to do that and finding it difficult, maybe you need to analyze any recent failures. What went wrong? Remember, if you are not failing regularly, you are not trying hard enough. The more times you fail at something, the closer you are to achieving a win. That said, make sure you are not making the same mistakes time and time again, or even twice. Analyze the situation honestly and write down what you think you could have done to prevent the failure. (Writing it down commits it to memory.) Why did you fail? Was it your attitude? If so, go to the chapters on passion, goal setting and staying motivated. Do you love what you are doing, or is it just a job? If it is just a job, you'll need to go back to your "why" for doing what you do, because passion is more important than any skill you can have.

Then rip up the paper, signifying that you forgive yourself for the failure. Now let it go.

Ever wake up in the middle of the night and replay something you are not happy or proud you did? You are not alone. We often replay our failures over and over, and it's not helpful.

There are two crucial things to do with failures: first, learn from them; second, don't repeat them.

What if you've done all this and the negative self-talk just won't stop? A good friend of mine calls her negative inner voice "Fang." Fang sits on her shoulder and constantly berates her.

If you have your own Fang, and I've never met anyone who doesn't, here are some strategies to help you get the better of it.

1. Name this negative voice. Feel free to co-opt Fang or use any another name that feels appropriate for you.

2. How do you recognize Fang? It's easy. It's any thought that makes you feel less than you are or tries to derail you from the goals you have set out for yourself. Don't let it get to you—think of Fang as a small dog barking ferociously at a leaf on the sidewalk.

3. Sometimes an event sets you back—life is never a smooth path. A wise friend would hug you and say something like, "I'm sorry you had to go through this, but it will pass, and I know you'll learn as much as there is to learn from it and put those lessons to good use." Fang says, "See, I told you so—you couldn't do it." When you hear that voice, stop. Mentally put Fang in its room and tell it you'll let it out when it's feeling more positive.

4. If you're having a difficult time ignoring Fang, ask a friend to help. Fang often comes in the night to list all the things we've done wrong in our lives and tell us what we should worry about now. We can usually dismiss this list in the morning—but be sure not to just hide it away for future use. By talking it through with a friend, you can deal with and dismiss each item, so Fang can't drag them out again!

5. If you speak to a friend about Fang (I guarantee they have a Fang of their own), you can also laugh about its ridiculously negative extremes with them. Next time it visits, just think about laughing with your friend, and lessen the power of its voice forever.

6. Post a sticky note somewhere you'll see it often, like on your laptop or mirror, with a sad face and the caption "DEFEAT FANG!" I know this sounds juvenile, but it works. We often let ourselves wander down a negative thought path, but if we catch ourselves in the early stages, it's much easier to do a quick course correction.

YOUR ACTION STEP

If you don't already meditate daily, download a meditation app such as Insight or Headspace onto your phone.

Even if you start with just a two-minute guided meditation each day, you are strengthening your brain, your resilience and your focus. (Don't be afraid to do it at work—you'll be modelling health for all the people you influence.)

Don't judge yourself for not meditating right—just do it. The only way you can fail is to give up. Once you have the two-minute meditation firmly entrenched in your daily habits, increase it to five minutes, and then 10.

TRANSFORMING FEAR INTO ENERGY

> Mom, sometimes fear grips me so hard
> I think I am going to faint!
> How do I get through it?

Let's face it: if you are not encountering fear in your business, you are not putting yourself outside of your comfort zone, which means you are not maximizing your potential. It's said all the time, and it can't be said enough: "If it were easy, everyone would do it!"

Fear is the body's natural response to a real or imagined threat, but the way you manage fear is a choice. You can choose to be shut down by the fear you're experiencing—or you can power through and overcome it.

Let me demonstrate this idea with a story about my most fear-filled experience, which happened on a trip to Mumbai in 2008. It was my first time in India, and I was super excited—even though I had been to many countries for my job by that point (42 in total), it was a dream-come-true opportunity.

I had a local sales rep, Sanket, and together we'd planned a 10-day, four-city trip to visit customers. After the first full day of sales calls, we ended up at the Taj Palace and Tower hotel in Mumbai. Sanket was a wonderful host, intent on making sure I saw lots of the region on our working tour. Looking back, I have to say that the hotel had a strange atmosphere—my briefcase was searched, and we had to go through metal detectors—but what did I know about India after one day? We had drinks in the bar and enjoyed the hotel's spectacular history and sights.

Later that evening, after we'd left, the Taj was attacked by a Pakistan-based terrorist group. At two in the morning, I was awoken by a call that made it very difficult to go back to sleep. To get as much worldwide media attention as possible, the terrorists chose target locations that were owned by international companies and were known for attracting people from overseas. I was staying in a hotel that met that description perfectly. Over the next four days, there would be 12 attacks throughout the city, killing 164 people and wounding over 300.

After telling me about the early attacks, the hotel concierge told me that the gated hotel was secured by a tank at the entrance but that we could be the next target. The city was under siege. He said the hotel had destroyed its copies of guest's passports so that the attackers wouldn't know I was Canadian if they did get into the hotel. I was told to pack, dress and watch what was happening on the minute-by-minute television news coverage of the bombings and shootings taking place throughout the city. I was also told not to open my door to anyone, and that the hotel would call first if they sent someone up for any reason.

It was now three a.m., and I was lying on my bed, fully clothed, watching the mayhem on TV. Was I scared? I was terrified.

But I knew I needed to remain calm or go absolutely mad in that small hotel room (with no mini bar!). Sanket called a couple of hours later to say how sorry he was, but at that moment, there was nothing he could do. Morning came, and the hotel sent up food. Other than the coffee, I could not touch a crumb. As I described it to someone later, the next three days were like a long, long roller coaster ride—sheer terror followed by moments of wondering what would happen next followed by sheer terror. On the second day, we were allowed out of our rooms, but there were still several terrorists at large. We were advised that we were at risk until they were found. I mingled with the other trapped guests, one a Swedish man who was always on the phone with his family. It was his first trip abroad, and he had a newborn baby at home. He couldn't even sit down. He paced back and forth, constantly checking the door to the hotel, expecting something to happen.

I was grateful I managed to keep it together, and I know it was my faith that helped. I couldn't imagine that this would be it—I felt there was so much more for me.

Most of the fear we experience is not triggered by events such as terrorist attacks, obviously, but by the things we face every day: giving a key presentation or taking a financial risk to grow our business. But it can feel the same—the part of our brain that governs fear is telling us our survival is at stake.

So how do we use this fear to spur us toward greatness?

First, see if you can transform your perception of even some the fear you feel into energy or even excitement. That's obviously easier in some situations than in others, but I can tell you, as I made my way to the recently reopened airport four days after I learned of the attacks, I was feeling pretty high. Not the kind of "things are a little fuzzy" high that is usually induced by sparkling wine, but an "I can do anything" high. Have you ever felt this way after an important meeting or presentation that had you stressed? Isn't that why we feel we have the right to celebrate after this kind of achievement?

How does it feel when you look back on the fear you felt, once you are on the other side? Easy, right? Well, okay, in my case it didn't seem easy, but it seemed a lot easier once I knew it was something I had survived.

It is often the unknown that intensifies our fear, the what-ifs that haunt us. How do we conquer those feelings? A great place to start is by educating yourself on all the facts, by being as prepared as possible. If I had had more confidence in the security experts around me in Mumbai, for example, I could have felt more comfortable. If you are presenting in front of a group of people, is it not much easier if you know your material inside and out?

Our brains are wired to automatically think the worst. Sometimes we even manufacture stories that cause us to worry—we "catastrophize" because some part of our brain thinks that imagining the worst possible outcome will help protect us. It rarely does, and it saps our energy and focus. It is important to recognize this when it starts happening and shut it down. Catastrophizing escalates anxiety and is almost never helpful. Remember that worrying is not the same as doing something. If you start to worry, use that energy to throw yourself into more preparation.

Fear has prevented more people from achieving greatness than almost anything else. How often are we talked out of going for that promotion or quitting our job to pursue our dreams?

Everyone experiences fear—it is what we do with it that counts. Cus D'Amato, the manager of three American Boxing Hall of Famers, said, "The hero and the coward both feel the same thing, but the hero projects it onto his opponent, while the coward runs." The idea that people can be fearless is a false concept: those who seem fearless are simply harnessing their fear to accomplish their goals.

Before I ran a marathon, I'd heard runners talk about the "wall" many times. When it happened to me, I was at mile 20, and I didn't feel like I could go on. I racked my brain trying to think of a way and started thinking about all the people I knew who had finished a marathon. I reminded myself that they were just normal people like me—nothing superhero about them, right? I wasn't going to give up, not when I had made it this far. As I thought about it, the solution came to me. I had run for about 10 minutes since I had thought I'd hit my wall, trying to work it all out, and I didn't die! As a matter of fact, I felt a bit better (not much, but a bit). I started making deals with myself: I will see how it feels when I get to that intersection, then decide.

My point is this: when you face these incredible fears, set some short-term goals. As it turned out, I made it through the next intersection and there was a beer station! As I said to myself, imagine if I had quit? I would have missed the beer! Dyson Inc. founder James Dyson said, "What I've learned from running is that the time to push hard is when you're hurting like crazy and you want to give up. Success is often just around the corner."

You are likely farther down the road with your project than you know. Celebrate. Congratulate yourself for your hard work and victories along the way, no matter how insignificant they seem. Speak positively to yourself.

I love this wise aphorism, usually credited to author and humorist Mark Twain: "Twenty years from now, you will be more disappointed by the things you didn't do than the ones you did. Throw off the bowlines. Sail away from the safe harbour. Catch the trade winds in your sails. Explore. Dream. Discover."

Every successful person you ask will give you the same advice: "Don't let fear stop you!"

YOUR ACTION STEP

HALT! Am I hungry, angry, lonely or tired?

Promise yourself you'll stop and ask this question whenever you feel unbearably fearful, anxious or stressed.

If the answer is yes, shift your focus. Don't try to problem-solve when you're not at your best. If you're hungry, eat. If you're angry, go for a walk or run. If you're lonely, call a friend. If you're tired, take a nap or, if that isn't possible, stick with menial, routine tasks until it's time to go to bed.

You'll be amazed at how often what seems to be an enormous, unsolvable, monstrous problem shrinks in size once you've taken care of your brain's basic needs.

MANAGING EXTREME STRESS BEFORE IT MANAGES YOU

Mom, there is so much pressure on me right now. It feels like the stress is eating me alive!

"Anxiety does not empty tomorrow of its sorrows, but only empties today of its strength."

CHARLES SPURGEON
English Baptist Pastor

"You are what you think you are ....
You become what you think about most of the time."

BRIAN TRACY
Author and Speaker

As many books and articles will tell you, stress is the new normal. You don't have to look very hard to see the toll it's taken on people in the Western world. The high cost of living, two-income families, budgets stretched to their limits and rampant misuse of credit have people running like hamsters on a wheel, just trying to keep up.

Unmanageable stress overload is a virus that takes hold of us, one that research has found creates untold damage to our health. It hijacks our thinking, our perception, our immune system and our ability to recover from setbacks.

In my case, it took panic attacks—20 years ago, when they weren't even in fashion—to wake me up to the fact that I was in trouble. I had two small kids (16 months apart), a full-time job and a third baby on the way. We were building a new home, managing the subcontractors ourselves and I was doing a part-time, three-year MBA program. What could go wrong?

I didn't see it coming. I was running through life on what seemed like the right path—certainly the path to success. Right?! Or was it?

I quickly found out when I ended up in the hospital in Palm Springs during a well-deserved and desperately needed week off. At 35 years of age, I was experiencing intense chest pains. What a wake-up call! At the time, the symptoms of panic attacks weren't widely recognized, so I was sent home after a heart attack was ruled out, told only that there was nothing wrong with my heart. I continued to have acute chest pains but didn't even tell my husband for fear he'd think I was crazy or a hypochondriac at the very least. It went on for two years until a naturopath finally diagnosed the panic attacks.

Then I had to ask myself a difficult question: "How did I get here?" I had everything I had ever wanted: three children, a career that was taking off, a brand-new house and a loving husband. Society told me I should be happy. But I wasn't, and I couldn't figure out what I could do to fix it. (Because I am a fixer, I always want to fix something.) It took a friend to pull me aside and explain to me that a) I didn't need to be everything to everyone and b) I needed help to find balance in my life. She also brought me to a Bible study.

With therapy and the introduction of faith into my life, I eventually worked my way out of my stressful situation. Some 20 years later, I still have to be careful of intense stress—I can feel the presence of a looming panic attack in certain situations and make adjustments when I feel it coming.

If you speak to any of my friends and family, they will tell you that I am one of the most laid-back, go-with-the-flow people they know. I know now that this type of person is very susceptible to anxiety and feelings of panic, as we hold everything in and second-guess everything going on around us. We take on the problems of the world and want to make sure everyone else is looked after.

Does any of this sound familiar?

Of course, women are the worst for this. It is the mother in us; our nurturing natures want to help the world, and so we tend to take on all the problems of those around us. In my therapy sessions, as I was going through this terrible time in my life, my therapist explained to me that there are givers and there are takers—many of the givers (those like me) tend to get panic attacks.

Before this experience, I thought I was too strong for stress, even though my mother suffered from mental illness and was hospitalized for it a few times. She took antidepressants, but depression was a constant compan-ion for her. I've since learned that many of the risk factors for depression and anxiety are hereditary and have recognized these factors in many of my family members as well.

Whether we have genetic risk factors or not, we are all vulnerable to depression and anxiety if we allow stress to overwhelm us. Especially if we are goal-oriented overachievers, we have to monitor ourselves for signs that stress is catching up with us.

Are you going through the motions, as I was, thinking it is what you are supposed to do—and not recognizing the symptoms that are trying desper-ately to tell you that something is wrong? Do you experience headaches, unexplained muscle or joint pain, irritability, insomnia or an inability to concentrate? Are you withdrawing from social situations and making excuses not to do some of the things you normally enjoy?

When I finally realized that things had to change, I'd reached a point where I wasn't even really enjoying my life anymore, and as I said, I had it all! It was not always bad, of course, but the bad days outweighed the good.

Does this sound like you? If so, it certainly does not mean there is something odd about you. You are human, and you are not alone! But you do need to make some changes, and you'll likely need help.

By evaluating your life—without guilt or shame and with the help of someone objective and compassionate, such as a therapist—you can get your life back on track. It isn't possible to eliminate stress, but you can reduce it. More importantly, you can recognize it and manage it, so it doesn't manage you.

Here are just some of the many, many common things that can stress us out. Learn to recognize them so you can stop stress from getting out of hand.

1. Procrastinating on work projects.

2. Putting off exercise and eating right.

3. Putting off dealing with difficult financial situations.

4. Being distracted by feelings of guilt, depression, laziness, loneliness and self-hatred.

5. Working towards the goals you've set for yourself without awareness that you can't do it all today.

Item #4 is huge. See "Overcoming Negativity" for strategies on wrestling this very human but intensively destructive habit to the ground.

YOUR ACTION STEP

Which of the five stress-inducers on the last page is the biggest challenge for you?

Take 10 minutes to make a list of possible action steps to address it, whether it is counselling, time management, "eating that frog," hiring a financial planner or finding an exercise buddy.

For extra credit, google "TED talk make stress your friend" for ideas on harnessing the upside of stress.

ON FINDING YOUR MOJO WHEN YOU FEEL LIKE GIVING UP

■ *Mom, I just feel like quitting!*

I hear you, my love, and as your mom, I'd like to give you a big hug and some ice cream.

As your business mentor, however, I need to deliver the hard news: positivity about what you are trying to accomplish is paramount.

Do you think the most successful people have it easy? Do you think success landed in their laps? This is so far from the truth. These are the people who refused to quit no matter what obstacles they faced—the people who refused to quit when they felt like quitting.

American evangelical pastor and author Rick Warren, leader of America's eighth-largest mega-church, said: "You are never a failure until you give up."

Worse, as renowned football coach Vince Lombardi famously said, "Once you learn to quit, it becomes a habit!"

It has been my experience that people often quit just before their breakthrough. If your mind is focused on the goal, you will make it!

Think about the source of your discouragement. Are you being overly influenced by naysayers, the people who try to convince us that what we are trying to do "has already been done" or, if it hasn't, that "it can't be done"? Or (I love this one the most!): "Why would you think you could be successful?" Remember that these people are trying to protect you or are trying to justify being stuck in a rut themselves, or possibly both. They're trying to convince you not to take risks because they don't have the drive or confidence to do so in their own lives. If you don't want their lives, don't allow yourself to be influenced by their fears. (Don't forget to revisit your sunshine file in these times and remember those who think you are doing great!)

Are you just worn out? It's so common among us driven types that the solution has even become a Pinterest meme, usually but not always attributed to famed anonymous public artist Banksy: "If you get tired, learn to rest, not to quit."

As an entrepreneur, it is inevitable that you will feel like quitting sometimes. The key here is to stay on track; stay positive. Prepare by having a list of things to do when you feel you can't go on or feel defeated. For me, it is motivational reading. (Again, take a look at the list at the back of the book.) Podcasts are also fabulous. Put your headphones on, choose one of the many suggestions you'll also find at the back of the book, and take a walk. Long or short—whatever works to get you out of the funk.

Whatever you do, don't make any rash decisions when you are in the thick of a problem that seems unresolvable. Give it time to pass. Sometimes, quitting is the right thing to do, but you'll know that when you feel positive, energized and confident—and ready for the next challenge, when you've discussed it with your biggest supporters and fans and come up with a new and even more exciting plan. Until then, hang in. Renew yourself and your energy.

1. Take a step back and give yourself some time to think by going for a walk. If you pray, meditate or do yoga, now's the time— these kinds of activities will get you grounded and reconnected with yourself.

2. Call your mom or a supportive friend who has your back and knows how to face risks and bounce back from discouragement.

3. Read some inspirational material, preferably some real-life stories about those who have overcome adversity to get to the top.

4. Get at least eight hours sleep tonight, preferably nine.

It may feel like quitting is the easiest way to stop feeling the way you're feeling, but it means going back to the beginning and giving up everything you've achieved to get as far as you have, doesn't it? Instead, go back to your goals and your "why," and you'll likely find lots of reasons quitting is not the best solution.

YOUR ACTION STEP

Think back to a time in your life when you really triumphed, when you felt smart, powerful and competent because you'd just demonstrated how smart, powerful and competent you are.

Maybe it was a test you aced or the time you learned to waterski in one day. Maybe it was a great presentation you gave or the tough sale you made.

Spend a few minutes remembering what it felt like. Try to remember the smells and sounds. Keep that feeling in your mental pocket for days like this.

WHEN PANIC
SETS IN

■ *Mom, I think my business is in trouble!*

I know I talk about gratitude a lot with you and your sisters and try to remind you often how privileged we are to live in the Western world. I think it's important to keep in mind, all the time—no matter what happens, we know we will not starve.

The situation you're going through is not easy, but just the fact you can read this book puts you in a better position than more than half of the people in the world.

It is hard, however, to continue to face adversity and remind yourself of these facts. Did you know that 71 percent of the world's population lives on less than $10 a day? For some of us, that is two trips to Starbucks!

Why am I wasting your time with this information when your business is in trouble? Because when we really are in trouble, we need some optimism. What I try to do is put each difficulty into perspective. Of course, we all love to throw around the "first-world problem" line, but do we fully internalize it?

Recognize the emotions of doubt, fear and anxiety that accompany any difficult business situation and don't panic.

Step back. Take a breath. Create a plan.

1. Are you bleeding cash with no end in sight? If so, sit down with your accountant and get the facts straight. Whatever you do, don't bury your head in the sand. Don't look back next month and realize you could have made some significant changes to get back on track. Do this now.

2. If you have a team, remember that it took that very same team to get you into this. And if they are good, they may very well get you out, too. Don't forget to communicate with them—there is no point in taking this on by yourself. Sit down with them to explain the situation and ask for constructive ideas. You will be surprised sometimes by where the great ideas come from. If you go this route, don't forget to seriously consider their suggestions!

3. Be open to criticism and make sure you own up to the mistakes of the past. Your team will shut down if you do not make this process safe for them.

4. Remember that opportunity often shows itself during challenging times. Most of us get too bogged down in the immediate difficulties to look for the opportunities that may be arising, so keep your eyes and ears open at all times.

5. Keep your vision in mind. Too often we panic and make reactive moves that are not in sync with our goals. If you have a mentor or coach, it is wise to discuss all options with her and get her take on the situation. If you don't, go to someone you trust and lay out the scenario. You might be totally off base, and it is good to get a reality check.

6. First and foremost, don't take yourself too seriously. Yes, the buck does stop with you, but taking the entire load on your shoulders is not a good use of your energy.

Finally, revisit your dream board and your goals. When you get to these times of uncertainty, you may need to be able to visually see what you are working on and why. Reignite your passion!

YOUR ACTION STEP

If you're reading this chapter because it's in the book and it's now its turn to be read, whew! Relax. You've just about finished the book—another accomplishment!! Yay, you! Now put it someplace handy, so you can reach for it when times get tough, because they will, and that's okay. You'll be ready.

If you're reading this chapter because your business is in trouble, though, this step is both urgent and important. It's your first priority. No matter what else is going on, whatever has to be cancelled, schedule some time today to go through the planning process described on the previous pages. If you can, pull in your team, your mentor, your accountant—all the firepower and resources you can get your hands on.

While you're going through the process, remember that regular breaks in nature are essential. Your solutions will only be as effective as your headspace.

THE END, FOR NOW

One of the most wonderful things about being an entrepreneur is that you never stop growing, learning, making mistakes and reaching higher.

In other words, I could have made this book 10 times as long and still not have shared everything I learned in my years in business. (Yes, that means this may be the first of many.)

But let me leave you with the four ideas I believe are the most essential to your success in the years to come.

First, find your tribe. Find people who inspire and support you, through networking or Facebook groups, your Chamber of Commerce or your place of worship. Having people to talk things through with and learn from makes all the difference.

On that note, I'm here for you if you need to chat. You can reach me through Instagram, Facebook or my website and we'll set up a time to talk. There is nothing that makes me happier than helping young women entrepreneurs uncover their personal genius and succeed.

Second, never give up. That doesn't mean you can't quit—not every idea is a good one. But know there is a huge difference between moving onto Plan B and surrendering to an obstacle that seems overwhelming. When you change course, make sure you're making that decision from a place of strength and calm.

Three, remember that it probably won't get done if it isn't in your calendar. Schedule everything that's important, even things like spending one-on-one time with your kids.

Finally, remember that whatever you build will only be as strong and resilient as you are. That means that taking care of yourself and your family can't be something you do "when you have time." In a busy life, if it isn't your first priority, it won't happen. And then your body will get your attention with illness, or your children will get your attention by acting out, or you'll realize your formerly loving partner has emotionally checked out.

Always remember: You can't build a strong business without building a strong you. And you never have to do either of those things alone.

Endnotes:

1. If you don't subscribe to *Entrepreneur*, you should: www.entrepreneur.com.

RESOURCES

Investing in your own learning
and personal growth is investing
in your future and your business.

For the richest possible life,
never stop.

Some of my favorite books, in no particular order:

- *The Slight Edge*, Jeff Olson

- *The Leader That Had No Title*, Robin Sharma

- *Screw It, Let's Do It*, Richard Branson

- *Secrets of Closing the Sale*, Zig Ziglar

- *Now Discover Your Strengths*, Marcus Buckingham and Donald Clifton

- *Who Moved My Cheese?* Spencer Johnson

- *Swim with the Sharks without Being Eaten Alive*, Harvey Mackay

- *How to Win Friends and Influence People*, Dale Carnegie

- *The 5 Second Rule*, Mel Robbins

- *Start with Why*, Simon Sinek

- *The Tipping Point*, Malcolm Gladwell

- Anything by Brian Tracy
  (You will find valuable lessons in all his books.)

- Anything by Tony Robbins
  (Any of Tony's books will start a fire under you.)

Podcasts that could make your life better:

- *The Goal Digger*

- *JLD On Fire*

- *Optimal Living Daily*

- *TED Talks Daily*

- *Tony Robbins podcast*

- *Success Unfiltered*

- *Oprah's SuperSoul Conversations*

- *The Sunny Show Podcast with Sunny Lenarduzzi*

- *Earn Your Happy*

- *Building a StoryBrand with Donald Miller*

- *Real Rebel Podcast*

- *Business Babes Collective*

- *The Knowledge Project*

HOPE International Development Agency

A portion of our profits will be donated to HOPE International Development Agency (HOPE International)—specifically to support women to provide for their families.

HOPE International exists to improve the supply of basic human necessities for the neediest of the developing world through self-help activities, and to challenge, educate, and involve North Americans regarding development issues.

Profits donated from this book will enable women in Ethiopia and India to join self-help groups, small groups of like-minded women in poor communities who come together to learn new skills, support each other in starting small businesses, and solve challenges faced by their community. HOPE International Development Agency will help these women develop a plan, borrow a small amount of money, and get to work making their dreams a reality.

These are basic but critical opportunities that will help families create long-term, self-sustaining change from poverty to self-reliance. Once they have established their businesses and are earning a regular income, they can return the loan to their self-help group, which will provide another family with a similar opportunity.

Consider yourself a partner in this effort. Thank you!

**HOPE International
Development Agency**